Frank Ormsby was born in Enniskillen in 1947 and was educated there at St Michael's College and later at Queen's University, Belfast. He is head of English at the Royal Belfast Academical Institution. In 1974 he won an Eric Gregory Award for his poetry, and his two collections, *A Store of Candles* (Oxford University Press, 1977; Gallery Press, 1986) and *A Northern Spring* (Secker & Warburg/Gallery Press, 1986), were both Poetry Book Society choices. He edited *Poets from the North of Ireland* (1979) and *Northern Windows: An Anthology of Ulster Autobiography* (1987), both published by Blackstaff Press, and he has been an editor of the *Honest Ulsterman* since 1969.

In memory of
John Hewitt

THE LONG EMBRACE

Twentieth Century Irish Love Poems

edited by

Frank Ormsby

THE
BLACKSTAFF
PRESS
BELFAST AND WOLFEBORO, NEW HAMPSHIRE

First published in 1987 by
The Blackstaff Press Limited
3 Galway Park, Dundonald, Belfast BT16 0AN, Northern Ireland
and
27 South Main Street, Wolfeboro, New Hampshire 03894 USA
with the assistance of
The Arts Council of Northern Ireland

© This collection, Blackstaff Press, 1987
© Foreword, Frank Ormsby, 1987
All rights reserved

Typeset by The Brown Fox

Printed by The Guernsey Press Limited

British Library Cataloguing in Publication Data

Ormsby, Frank
The Long embrace: twentieth-century Irish love poems.
1. English poetry – Irish authors 2. Love poetry, English
I. Title
821'.912'080354 PR6110.L6

Library of Congress Cataloging-in-Publication Data
The Long embrace
Includes index.
1. Love poetry, English – Irish authors. 2. English poetry – 20th century. 3. Ireland – Poetry.
I. Ormsby, Frank, 1947-
PR8861.L6L66 1987 821'.91'080354 87-18247

ISBN 0-85640-387-3

CONTENTS

FOREWORD

> A year ago I fell in love with the functional ward
> Of a chest hospital . . .

wrote Patrick Kavanagh, reminding us that there can be no simple definition of what constitutes a 'love poem'. Kavanagh went on to assert that 'nothing whatever is by love debarred', a passionate, euphoric generalisation, perhaps, yet it would not be difficult to compile a list of poems about family, childhood, animals, landscape, the city, travel, art and music, for example, to which the term 'love poetry' could appropriately be applied. The pity and anger in many 'war' poems are fuelled by love, as are the impulses and intentions underlying much satirical verse, and the term certainly describes most 'religious' poetry.

This anthology is devoted primarily to romantic and erotic love in many of their complex combinations and manifestations. The title is taken from Frank O'Connor's translation from the Irish, 'A History of Love' (*c*.1600), in which, among a number of innovative lovers, the 'son of Conall' is said to have 'left us in his debt/By figuring the long embrace.' In the context of the poem, the phrase connotes affection and ardent physical contact; out of context, it might, in addition, suggest love gone past its prime, an entanglement from which release is craved; and its place in a modern translation of a four-hundred-year-old poem is a reminder of the long fruitful embrace of the Irish and English literary traditions.

So the poems collected here range timelessly over the joys and miseries of the love experience. They are tender, passionate, bawdy and reverential. They embody delight, pleasure, longing, frustration, jealousy, fear, pain, grief and guilt. Some are emotionally circumspect, others uninhibitedly direct. Most engagingly, it seems to me, they present the sturdiness, the fragility, the transforming power of love in its everyday, familiar settings and circumstances: love as it flourishes – or fails to flourish – in youth and old age, indoors and out, inside and outside marriage; love in the vicinity of the toaster, the washing machine, the baking bowl, the ironing board, the Turkish carpet and the home brew; love by a window in Paris, by a hospital bed; love as an ardent celebration of the living and a poignant remembrance of the dead; love in the back seat of a Datsun, love attempted on tiptoe on a copy of Dickens's *Our Mutual Friend*; love as a sharing of caresses, love ending in blows; love in the railway station and the departure lounge, in a 'London littered with remembered kisses' and in the grass outside Áras an Uachtaráin, in letters, in dreams, in the personal columns of newspapers, in car parks and hotel rooms; love for the first time and after many failures; love in time of war; love as it is trammelled by and defies the puritanical dictates of church and state.

Musically formal, colloquially vigorous, imagistically rich and suggestive, meditatively restrained, these poems, in their different ways,

> . . . record love's mystery without claptrap,
> Snatch out of time the passionate transitory.

Frank Ormsby, 1987

W.B. YEATS
1865–1939

NEVER GIVE ALL THE HEART

Never give all the heart, for love
Will hardly seem worth thinking of
To passionate women if it seem
Certain, and they never dream
That it fades out from kiss to kiss;
For everything that's lovely is
But a brief, dreamy, kind delight.
O never give the heart outright,
For they, for all smooth lips can say,
Have given their hearts up to the play.
And who could play it well enough
If deaf and dumb and blind with love?
He that made this knows all the cost,
For he gave all his heart and lost.

A DRINKING SONG

Wine comes in at the mouth
And love comes in at the eye;
That's all we shall know for truth
Before we grow old and die.
I lift the glass to my mouth,
I look at you, and I sigh.

BROWN PENNY

I whispered, 'I am too young,'
And then, 'I am old enough';
Wherefore I threw a penny

To find out if I might love.
'Go and love, go and love, young man,
If the lady be young and fair.'
Ah, penny, brown penny, brown penny,
I am looped in the loops of her hair.

O love is the crooked thing,
There is nobody wise enough
To find out all that is in it,
For he would be thinking of love
Till the stars had run away
And the shadows eaten the moon.
Ah, penny, brown penny, brown penny,
One cannot begin it too soon.

FRIENDS

Now must I these three praise –
Three women that have wrought
What joy is in my days:
One because no thought,
Nor those unpassing cares,
No, not in these fifteen
Many-times-troubled years,
Could ever come between
Mind and delighted mind;
And one because her hand
Had strength that could unbind
What none can understand,
What none can have and thrive,
Youth's dreamy load, till she
So changed me that I live
Labouring in ecstasy.
And what of her that took
All till my youth was gone
With scarce a pitying look?

How could I praise that one?
When day begins to break
I count my good and bad,
Being wakeful for her sake,
Remembering what she had,
What eagle look still shows,
While up from my heart's root
So great a sweetness flows
I shake from head to foot.

MEMORY

One had a lovely face,
And two or three had charm,
But charm and face were in vain
Because the mountain grass
Cannot but keep the form
Where the mountain hare has lain.

HER PRAISE

She is foremost of those that I would hear praised.
I have gone about the house, gone up and down
As a man does who has published a new book,
Or a young girl dressed out in her new gown,
And though I have turned the talk by hook or crook
Until her praise should be the uppermost theme,
A woman spoke of some new tale she had read,
A man confusedly in a half dream
As though some other name ran in his head.
She is foremost of those that I would hear praised.

I will talk no more of books or the long war
But walk by the dry thorn until I have found
Some beggar sheltering from the wind, and there

Manage the talk until her name come round.
If there be rags enough he will know her name
And be well pleased remembering it, for in the old days,
Though she had young men's praise and old men's blame,
Among the poor both old and young gave her praise.

BROKEN DREAMS

There is grey in your hair.
Young men no longer suddenly catch their breath
When you are passing;
But maybe some old gaffer mutters a blessing
Because it was your prayer
Recovered him upon the bed of death.
For your sole sake – that all heart's ache have known,
And given to others all heart's ache,
From meagre girlhood's putting on
Burdensome beauty – for your sole sake
Heaven has put away the stroke of her doom,
So great her portion in that peace you make
By merely walking in a room.

Your beauty can but leave among us
Vague memories, nothing but memories.
A young man when the old men are done talking
Will say to an old man, 'Tell me of that lady
The poet stubborn with his passion sang us
When age might well have chilled his blood.'

Vague memories, nothing but memories,
But in the grave all, all, shall be renewed.
The certainty that I shall see that lady
Leaning or standing or walking
In the first loveliness of womanhood,
And with the fervour of my youthful eyes,
Has set me muttering like a fool.

You are more beautiful than any one,
And yet your body had a flaw:
Your small hands were not beautiful,
And I am afraid that you will run
And paddle to the wrist
In the mysterious, always brimming lake
Where those that have obeyed the holy law
Paddle and are perfect. Leave unchanged
The hands that I have kissed,
For old sake's sake.

The last stroke of midnight dies.
All day in the one chair
From dream to dream and rhyme to rhyme I have ranged
In rambling talk with an image of air:
Vague memories, nothing but memories.

LULLABY

Beloved, may your sleep be sound
That have found it where you fed.
What were all the world's alarms
To mighty Paris when he found
Sleep upon a golden bed
That first dawn in Helen's arms?

Sleep, beloved, such a sleep
As did that wild Tristram know
When, the potion's work being done,
Roe could run or doe could leap
Under oak and beechen bough,
Roe could leap or doe could run;

Such a sleep and sound as fell
Upon Eurotas' grassy bank
When the holy bird, that there

Accomplished his predestined will,
From the limbs of Leda sank
But not from her protecting care.

AFTER LONG SILENCE

Speech after long silence; it is right,
All other lovers being estranged or dead,
Unfriendly lamplight hid under its shade,
The curtains drawn upon unfriendly night,
That we descant and yet again descant
Upon the supreme theme of Art and Song:
Bodily decrepitude is wisdom; young
We loved each other and were ignorant.

FATHER AND CHILD

She hears me strike the board and say
That she is under ban
Of all good men and women,
Being mentioned with a man
That has the worst of all bad names;
And thereupon replies
That his hair is beautiful,
Cold as the March wind his eyes.

A LAST CONFESSION

What lively lad most pleasured me
Of all that with me lay?
I answer that I gave my soul
And loved in misery,

But had great pleasure with a lad
That I loved bodily.

Flinging from his arms I laughed
To think his passion such
He fancied that I gave a soul
Did but our bodies touch,
And laughed upon his breast to think
Beast gave beast as much.

I gave what other women gave
That stepped out of their clothes,
But when this soul, its body off,
Naked to naked goes,
He it has found shall find therein
What none other knows,

And give his own and take his own
And rule in his own right;
And though it loved in misery
Close and cling so tight,
There's not a bird of day that dare
Extinguish that delight.

POLITICS

In our time the destiny of man presents
its meaning in political terms.
THOMAS MANN

How can I, that girl standing there,
My attention fix
On Roman or on Russian
Or on Spanish politics?
Yet here's a travelled man that knows
What he talks about,

And there's a politician
That has read and thought,
And maybe what they say is true
Of war and war's alarms,
But O that I were young again
And held her in my arms!

J.M. SYNGE

1871–1909

DREAD

Beside a chapel I'd a room looked down,
Where all the women from the farms and town,
On holy days, and Sundays used to pass
To marriages, and christenings and to Mass.

Then I sat lonely watching score and score,
Till I turned jealous of the Lord next door . . .
Now by this window, where there's none can see,
The Lord God's jealous of yourself and me.

A QUESTION

I asked if I got sick and died, would you
With my black funeral go walking too,
If you'd stand close to hear them talk or pray
While I'm let down in that steep bank of clay.

And, No, you said, for if you saw a crew
Of living idiots, pressing round that new
Oak coffin – they alive, I dead beneath
That board – you'd rave and rend them with your teeth.

PADRAIC COLUM

1881–1972

SHE MOVED THROUGH THE FAIR

My young love said to me, 'My brothers won't mind,
And my parents won't slight you for your lack of kind.'
Then she stepped away from me, and this she did say,
'It will not be long, love, till our wedding day.'

She stepped away from me and she moved through the fair,
And fondly I watched her go here and go there,
Then she went her way homeward with one star awake,
As the swan in the evening moves over the lake.

The people were saying no two were e'er wed
But one had a sorrow that never was said,
And I smiled as she passed with her goods and her gear,
And that was the last that I saw of my dear.

I dreamt it last night that my young love came in,
So softly she entered, her feet made no din;
She came close beside me, and this she did say,
'It will not be long, love, till our wedding day.'

O WOMAN, SHAPELY AS THE SWAN

O woman, shapely as the swan,
On your account I shall not die:
The men you've slain – a trivial clan –
Were less than I.

I ask me shall I die for these –
For blossom teeth and scarlet lips –

And shall that delicate swan-shape
Bring me eclipse?

Well-shaped the breasts and smooth the skin,
The cheeks are fair, the tresses free –
And yet I shall not suffer death,
God over me!

Those even brows, that hair like gold,
Those languorous tones, that virgin way,
The flowing limbs, the rounded heel
Slight men betray!

Thy spirit keen through radiant mien,
Thy shining throat and smiling eye,
Thy little palm, thy side like foam –
I cannot die!

O woman, shapely as the swan,
In a cunning house hard-reared was I:
O bosom white, O well-shaped palm,
I shall not die!

AFTER THE IRISH (Anonymous, 15th–16th centuries)

AUSTIN CLARKE
1896–1974

THE PLANTER'S DAUGHTER

When night stirred at sea
And the fire brought a crowd in,
They say that her beauty
Was music in mouth
And few in the candlelight
Thought her too proud,
For the house of the planter
Is known by the trees.

Men that had seen her
Drank deep and were silent,
The women were speaking
Wherever she went –
As a bell that is rung
Or a wonder told shyly
And O she was the Sunday
In every week.

THE STRAYING STUDENT

On a holy day when sails were blowing southward,
A bishop sang the Mass at Inishmore,
Men took one side, their wives were on the other
But I heard the woman coming from the shore:
And wild in despair my parents cried aloud
For they saw the vision draw me to the doorway.

Long had she lived in Rome when popes were bad,
The wealth of every age she makes her own,
Yet smiled on me in eager admiration,

And for a summer taught me all I know,
Banishing shame with her great laugh that rang
As if a pillar caught it back alone.

I learned the prouder counsel of her throat,
My mind was growing bold as light in Greece;
And when in sleep her stirring limbs were shown,
I blessed the noonday rock that knew no tree:
And for an hour the mountain was her throne,
Although her eyes were bright with mockery.

They say I was sent back from Salamanca
And failed in logic, but I wrote her praise
Nine times upon a college wall in France.
She laid her hand at darkfall on my page
That I might read the heavens in a glance
And I knew every star the Moors had named.

Awake or in my sleep, I have no peace now,
Before the ball is struck, my breath has gone,
And yet I tremble lest she may deceive me
And leave me in this land, where every woman's son
Must carry his own coffin and believe,
In dread, all that the clergy teach the young.

PENAL LAW

Burn Ovid with the rest. Lovers will find
A hedge-school for themselves and learn by heart
All that the clergy banish from the mind,
When hands are joined and head bows in the dark.

THE ENVY OF POOR LOVERS

Pity poor lovers who may not do what they please
With their kisses under a hedge, before a raindrop

Unhouses it; and astir from wretched centuries,
Bramble and briar remind them of the saints.

Her envy is the curtain seen at night-time,
Happy position that could change her name.
His envy – clasp of the married whose thoughts can be alike,
Whose nature flows without the blame or shame.

Lying in the grass as if it were a sin
To move, they hold each other's breath, tremble,
Ready to share that ancient dread – kisses begin
Again – of Ireland keeping company with them.

Think, children, of institutions mured above
Your ignorance, where every look is veiled,
State-paid to snatch away the folly of poor lovers
For whom, it seems, the sacraments have failed.

MONK GIBBON

b. 1896

L'AMITIÉ

She allows me kiss her twice, as though to say,
'Yes, my entire good will is yours, my friend.
We understand each other: or, at least,
We strive to make our mutual mystery end.'

But nothing ends that mystery. My thoughts
Go back to when – comparative strangers – we
Discussed a dozen earnest trifles, yet
Endowed them with a strange intensity;

And how weeks later, once, I saw you come
Into a room, dressed for some grand affair
In silk, and for ten minutes could admire
The straight division in your well-brushed hair,

And feel, 'She's lovely, very lovely. Men
Have turned less loveliness than this to rhyme.'
Yet, never, in the craziest flight of hope,
Imagined, then, that there could come a time

When we would kiss as friends. But now I see
Kisses, or even love itself, must be
Almost, and to the very end, mere balm
Given to assuage that mutual mystery.

Children stand tiptoe at a fence of wood,
And all they glimpse seems as by magic made:
So, in the lovely tumult of our days,
The heart stands tiptoe at its palisade.

I TELL HER SHE IS LOVELY

I tell her she is lovely and she laughs,
Shy laughter altogether lovely too;
Knowing, perhaps that it was true before;
And, when she laughs, that it is still more true.

PATRICK MacDONAGH

1902–1961

BE STILL AS YOU ARE BEAUTIFUL

Be still as you are beautiful
Be silent as the rose;
Through miles of starlit countryside
Unspoken worship flows
To reach you in your loveless room
From lonely men whom daylight gave
The blessing of your passing face
Impenetrably grave.

A white owl in the lichened wood
Is circling silently,
More secret and more silent yet
Must be your love to me.
Thus, while about my dreaming head
Your soul in ceaseless vigil goes,
Be still as you are beautiful
Be silent as the rose.

SHE WALKED UNAWARE

O, she walked unaware of her own increasing beauty
That was holding men's thoughts from market or plough,
As she passed by intent on her womanly duties
And she without leisure to be wayward or proud;
Or if she had pride then it was not in her thinking
But thoughtless in her body like a flower of good breeding.
The first time I saw her spreading coloured linen
Beyond the green willow she gave me gentle greeting
With no more intention than the leaning willow tree.

Though she smiled without intention yet from that day forward
Her beauty filled like water the four corners of my being,
And she rested in my heart like a hare in the form
That is shaped to herself. And I that would be singing
Or whistling at all times went silently then;
Till I drew her aside among straight stems of beeches
When the blackbird was sleeping, and she promised that never
The fields would be ripe but I'd gather all sweetness,
A red moon of August would rise on our wedding.

October is spreading bright flame along stripped willows
Low fires of the dogwood burn down to grey water –
God pity me now and all desolate sinners
Demented with beauty! I have blackened my thought
In drouths of bad longing, and all brightness goes shrouded
Since he came with his rapture of wild words that mirrored
Her beauty and made her ungentle and proud.
Tonight she will spread her brown hair on his pillow
But I shall be hearing the harsh cries of wild fowl.

FRANK O'CONNOR
1903–1966

A HISTORY OF LOVE

This is Love's history
And how it all began:
As an authority
I am your foremost man.

Diarmuid the bold and gay,
Chief of the warrior bands,
With Grania one day
Invented holding hands.

While Ulster's Hound as well,
When a Greek girl went by,
Falling beneath her spell,
Was first with the glad eye.

Naisi, home from the chase,
Weary, inspired with bliss,
Seeing Deirdre don her trews,
Endowed us with the kiss.

The son of Conall met
Their challenges with grace
And left us in his debt
By figuring the long embrace.

Avartach, king of the fairies,
Following in their track,
With his arbutus berries
Put a girl upon her back.

Ceadach, master of trades,
Seeing them still unversed –
Those white-skinned Irish maids –
Made women of them first.

And Angus as they say –
Lord of the Sacred Hill –
First took their clothes away,
And gave them perfect skill.

Learning that hearts can break
Under Love's miseries
Beside a Munster lake,
Glas filled the air with sighs.

Lamenting to soft strings
And moans upon the pipe,
Were Mongan's offering
To woo some timid wife.

But I to my own grief,
First open Jealousy's door –
This is my tale in brief –
And now it shuts no more.

AFTER THE IRISH (Anonymous, 17th century)

A LEARNED MISTRESS

Tell him it's all a lie;
I love him as much as my life;
He needn't be jealous of me –
I love him and loathe his wife.

If he kill me through jealousy now
His wife will perish of spite,

He'll die of grief for his wife –
Three of us dead in a night.

All blessings from heaven to earth
On the head of the woman I hate,
And the man I love as my life,
Sudden death be his fate.

AFTER THE IRISH (Anonymous, 13th–17th centuries)

THE BODY'S SPEECH

My grief, my grief, maid without sin,
Mother of God's Son,
Because of one I cannot win
My peace is gone.

Mortal love, a raging flood,
O Mother Maid,
Runs like a fever through my blood,
Ruins heart and head.

How can I tell her of my fear,
My wild desire,
When words I speak for my own ear
Turn me to fire?

I dream of breasts so lily-like,
Without a fleck,
And hair that, bundled up from her back,
Burdens her neck.

And praise the cheeks where flames arise
That shame the rose,
And the soft hands at whose touch flees
All my repose.

Since I have seen her I am lost,
A man possessed,
Better to feel the world gone past,
Earth on my breast;

And from my tomb to hear the choir,
The hum of prayer;
Without her while her place is here,
My peace is there.

I am a ghost upon your path,
A wasting death,
But you must know one word of truth
Gives a ghost breath –

In language beyond learning's touch
Passion can teach –
Speak in that speech beyond reproach,
The body's speech.

AFTER THE IRISH of Donal MacCarthy More,
Earl Clancarthy, 16th century

from THE LAMENT FOR ART O'LEARY

My love and my mate
That I never thought dead
Till your horse came to me
With bridle trailing,
All blood from forehead
To polished saddle
Where you should be,
Either sitting or standing;
I gave one leap to the threshold,

A second to the gate,
A third upon its back.

I clapped my hands,
And off at a gallop;
I never lingered
Till I found you lying
By a little furze-bush
Without pope or bishop
Or priest or cleric
One prayer to whisper
But an old, old woman,
And her cloak about you,
And your blood in torrents –
Art O'Leary –
I did not wipe it off,
I drank it from my palms.

My love and my delight
Stand up now beside me,
And let me lead you home
Until I make a feast,
And I will roast the meat
And send for company
And call the harpers in,
And I shall make your bed
Of soft and snowy sheets
And blankets dark and rough
To warm the beloved limbs
An autumn blast has chilled.

AFTER THE IRISH of Eileen O'Leary, 18th century

ADVICE TO LOVERS

The way to get on with a girl
Is to drift like a man in a mist,
Happy enough to be caught,
Happy to be dismissed.

Glad to be out of her way,
Glad to rejoin her in bed,
Equally grieved or gay
To learn that she's living or dead.

AFTER THE IRISH (Anonymous, 7th–12th centuries)

GEORGE BUCHANAN
b. 1904

I SUDDENLY . . .

I suddenly have come to love
you who have been no more than friend
so long and constantly . . .
                                    I am
a traveller startled that the end
of stormy questing in a ship
for lands of mystery should be
to sight the blue smoke of his home
and anchor at his native quay.

SONG FOR STRAPHANGERS

I bought a red-brick villa
   and dug the garden round
because a young girl smiled in June:
   in August we were bound
      by a marriage vow,
      and then till now
I count up every pound.

I count up every penny,
   I work and never cease,
because a young girl smiled in June
   and there is no release.
      Sometimes I swear
      it's most unfair.
Sometimes I feel at peace.

PATRICK KAVANAGH

1904–1967

BLUEBELLS FOR LOVE

There will be bluebells growing under the big trees
And you will be there and I will be there in May;
For some other reason we both will have to delay
The evening in Dunshaughlin – to please
Some imagined relation,
So both of us came to walk through that plantation.

We will be interested in the grass,
In an old bucket-hoop, in the ivy that weaves
Green incongruity among dead leaves,
We will put on surprise at carts that pass –
Only sometimes looking sideways at the bluebells in the plantation
And never frighten them with too wild an exclamation.

We will be wise, we will not let them guess
That we are watching them or they will pose
A mere façade like boys
Caught out in virtue's naturalness.
We will not impose on the bluebells in that plantation
Too much of our desire's adulation.

We will have other loves – or so they'll think;
The primroses or the ferns or the briars,
Or even the rusty paling wires,
Or the violets on the sunless sorrel bank.
Only as an aside the bluebells in the plantation
Will mean a thing to our dark contemplation.

We'll know love little by little, glance by glance.
Ah, the clay under these roots is so brown!
We'll steal from heaven while God is in the town –

I caught an angel smiling in a chance
Look through the tree-trunks of the plantation
As you and I walked slowly to the station.

THE HOSPITAL

A year ago I fell in love with the functional ward
Of a chest hospital: square cubicles in a row
Plain concrete, wash basins – an art lover's woe,
Not counting how the fellow in the next bed snored.
But nothing whatever is by love debarred,
The common and banal her heat can know.
The corridor led to a stairway and below
Was the inexhaustible adventure of a gravelled yard.

This is what love does to things: the Rialto Bridge,
The main gate that was bent by a heavy lorry,
The seat at the back of a shed that was a suntrap.
Naming these things is the love-act and its pledge;
For we must record love's mystery without claptrap,
Snatch out of time the passionate transitory.

PADRAIC FALLON
1905–1974

MARY HYNES

That Sunday, on my oath, the rain was a heavy overcoat
On a poor poet, and when the rain began
In fleeces of water to buckleap like a goat
I was only a walking penance reaching Kiltartan;
And there, so suddenly that my cold spine
Broke out on the arch of my back in a rainbow,
This woman surged out of the day with so much sunlight
I was nailed there like a scarecrow,

But I found my tongue and the breath to balance it
And I said: 'If I bow to you with this hump of rain
I'll fall on my collarbone, but look, I'll chance it,
And after falling, bow again.'
She laughed, ah, she was gracious, and softly she said to me,
'For all your lovely talking I go marketing with an ass,
I'm no hill-queen, alas, or Ireland, that grass widow,
So hurry on, sweet Raftery, or you'll keep me late for Mass!'

The parish priest has blamed me for missing second Mass
And the bell talking on the rope of the steeple,
But the tonsure of the poet is the bright crash
Of love that blinds the irons on his belfry,
Were I making an *aisling* I'd tell the tale of her hair,
But now I've grown careful of my listeners
So I pass over one long day and the rainy air
Where we sheltered in whispers.

When we left the dark evening at last outside her door,
She lighted a lamp though a gaming company
Could have sighted each trump by the light of her unshawled poll,
And indeed she welcomed me

With a big quart bottle and I mooned there over glasses
Till she took that bird, the phoenix, from the spit;
And 'Raftery,' says she, 'a feast is no bad dowry,
Sit down now and taste it!'

If I praised Ballylea before it was only for the mountains
Where I broke horses and ran wild,
And not for its seven crooked smoky houses
Where seven crones are tied
All day to the listening top of a half-door,
And nothing to be heard or seen
But the drowsy dropping of water
And a gander on the green.

But, boys! I was blind as a kitten till last Sunday.
This town is earth's very navel!
Seven palaces are thatched there of a Monday,
And O the seven queens whose pale
Proud faces with their seven glimmering sisters,
The Pleiades, light the evening where they stroll,
And one can find the well by their wet footprints,
And make one's soul;

For Mary Hynes, rising, gathers up there
Her ripening body from all the love stories;
And, rinsing herself at morning, shakes her hair
And stirs the old gay books in libraries;
And what shall I do with sweet Boccaccio?
And shall I send Ovid back to school again
With a new headline for his copybook,
And a new pain?

Like a nun she will play you a sweet tune on a spinet,
And from such grasshopper music leap
Like Herod's hussy who fancied a saint's head
For grace after meat;
Yet she'll peg out a line of clothes on a windy morning

And by noonday put them ironed in the chest,
And you'll swear by her white fingers she does nothing
But take her fill of rest.

And I'll wager now that my song is ended,
Loughrea, that old dead city where the weavers
Have pined at the mouldering looms since Helen broke the thread,
Will be piled again with silver fleeces:
O the new coats and big horses! The raving and the ribbons!
And Ballylea in hubbub and uproar!
And may Raftery be dead if he's not there to ruffle it
On his own mare, shank's mare, that never needs a spur!

But ah, Sweet Light, though your face coins
My heart's very metals, isn't it folly without pardon
For Raftery to sing so that men, east and west, come
Spying on your vegetable garden?
We could be so quiet in your chimney corner –
Yet how could a poet hold you any more than the sun,
Burning in the big bright hazy heart of harvest,
Could be tied in a hen run?

Bless your poet then and let him go!
He'll never stack a haggard with his breath:
His thatch of words will not keep rain or snow
Out of the house, or keep back death.
But Raftery, rising, curses as he sees you
Stir the fire and wash delph,
That he was bred a poet whose selfish trade it is
To keep no beauty to himself.

AFTER THE IRISH of Anthony Raftery, 18th–19th centuries

SAMUEL BECKETT

b. 1906

I WOULD LIKE MY LOVE TO DIE

I would like my love to die
and the rain to be raining on the graveyard
and on me walking the streets
mourning her who thought she loved me.

JOHN HEWITT
1907–1987

ET TU IN ARCADIA VIXISTI
for Roberta

You woke me, rising – this in Paris once –
I watched you stepping – thirty years ago –
to the long window – Many such we've since
unshuttered back from narrow streets below,
but on no more than stir of wheel or foot –
as, finger-signalled, following, I stood
beside you, heeding, drifting up, a flute-
like music, blown through the clean hollow wood,
while, leaning, a dark lad against the wall
played to the splay of goats about his knees,
strayed, so it seemed, from classic pastoral,
an instant's magic – never ours in Greece,
when, later, older, or in Sicily,
we stood, at dawn, beside the tideless sea.

from
SONNETS FOR ROBERTA
(1954)

I

How have I served you? I have let you waste
the substance of your summer on my mood;
the image of the woman is defaced,
and some mere chattel-thing of cloth and wood
performs the household rites, while I, content,
mesh the fine words to net the turning thought,
or eke the hours out, gravely diligent,

to draw to sight that which, when it is brought,
is seldom worth the labour, while you wait,
the little loving gestures held at bay,
each mocking moment inappropriate
for pompous duty never stoops to play;
yet sometimes, at a pause, I recognise
the lonely pity in your lifted eyes.

II

If I had given you that love and care
I long have lavished with harsh loyalty
on some blurred concept spun of earth and air
and real only in some bird or tree,
then you had lived in every pulse and tone
and found the meaning in the wine and bread
who have been forced to walk these ways alone,
my dry thoughts droning always on ahead.
Then had you lived as other women live,
warmed by a touch, responsive to a glance,
glad to endure, so that endurance give
the right to share each changing circumstance,
and yet, for all my treason, you were true
to me, as I to something less than you.

LOUIS MacNEICE

1907–1963

MAYFLY

Barometer of my moods today, mayfly,
Up and down one among a million, one
The same at best as the rest of the jigging mayflies,
One only day of May alive beneath the sun.

The yokels tilt their pewters and the foam
Flowers in the sun beside the jewelled water.
Daughter of the South, call the sunbeams home
To nest between your breasts. The kingcups
Ephemeral are gay gulps of laughter.

Gulp of yellow merriment; cackle of ripples;
Lips of the river that pout and whisper round the reeds.
The mayfly flirting and posturing over the water
Goes up and down in the lift so many times for fun.

'When we are grown up we are sure to alter
Much for the better, to adopt solider creeds;
The kingcup will cease proffering his cup
And the foam will have blown from the beer and the heat no
  longer dance
And the lift lose fascination and the May
Change her tune to June – but the trouble with us mayflies
Is that we never have the chance to be grown up.'

They never have the chance, but what of time they have
They stretch out taut and thin and ringing clear;
So we, whose strand of life is not much more,
Let us too make our time elastic and
Inconsequently dance above the dazzling wave.

Nor put too much on the sympathy of things,
The dregs of drink, the dried cups of flowers,
The pathetic fallacy of the passing hours
When it is we who pass them – hours of stone,
Long rows of granite sphinxes looking on.

It is we who pass them, we the circus masters
Who make the mayflies dance, the lapwings lift their crests,
The show will soon shut down, its gay-rags gone,
But when this summer is over let us die together,
I want always to be near your breasts.

THE SUNLIGHT ON THE GARDEN

The sunlight on the garden
Hardens and grows cold,
We cannot cage the minute
Within its nets of gold,
When all is told
We cannot beg for pardon.

Our freedom as free lances
Advances towards its end;
The earth compels, upon it
Sonnets and birds descend;
And soon, my friend,
We shall have no time for dances.

The sky was good for flying
Defying the church bells
And every evil iron
Siren and what it tells:
The earth compels,
We are dying, Egypt, dying

And not expecting pardon,
Hardened in heart anew,
But glad to have sat under
Thunder and rain with you,
And grateful too
For sunlight on the garden.

from TRILOGY FOR X

II

And love hung still as crystal over the bed
  And filled the corners of the enormous room;
The boom of dawn that left her sleeping, showing
  The flowers mirrored in the mahogany table.

O my love, if only I were able
  To protract this hour of quiet after passion,
Not ration happiness but keep this door for ever
  Closed on the world, its own world closed within it.

But dawn's waves trouble with the bubbling minute,
  The names of books come clear upon their shelves,
The reason delves for duty and you will wake
  With a start and go on living on your own.

The first train passes and the windows groan,
  Voices will hector and your voice become
A drum in tune with theirs, which all last night
  Like sap that fingered through a hungry tree
Asserted our one night's identity.

from AUTUMN JOURNAL

IV

September has come and I wake
   And I think with joy how whatever, now or in future, the
      system
Nothing whatever can take
   The people away, there will always be people
For friends or for lovers though perhaps
   The conditions of love will be changed and its vices
      diminished
And affection not lapse
   To narrow possessiveness, jealousy founded on vanity.
September has come, it is *hers*
   Whose vitality leaps in the autumn,
Whose nature prefers
   Trees without leaves and a fire in the fire-place;
So I give her this month and the next
   Though the whole of my year should be hers who has
      rendered already
So many of its days intolerable or perplexed
   But so many more so happy;
Who has left a scent on my life and left my walls
   Dancing over and over with her shadow,
Whose hair is twined in all my waterfalls
   And all of London littered with remembered kisses.
So I am glad
   That life contains her with her moods and moments
More shifting and more transient than I had
   Yet thought of as being integral to beauty;
Whose mind is like the wind on a sea of wheat,
   Whose eyes are candour,
And assurance in her feet
   Like a homing pigeon never by doubt diverted.
To whom I send my thanks
   That the air has become shot silk, the streets are music,
And that the ranks

Of men are ranks of men, no more of cyphers.
So that if now alone
I must pursue this life, it will not be only
A drag from numbered stone to numbered stone
But a ladder of angels, river turning tidal.
Off-hand, at times hysterical, abrupt,
You are one I always shall remember,
Whom cant can never corrupt
Nor argument disinherit.
Frivolous, always in a hurry, forgetting the address
Frowning too often, taking enormous notice
Of hats and backchat – how could I assess
The thing that makes you different?
You whom I remember glad or tired,
Smiling in drink or scintillating anger,
Inopportunely desired
On boats, on trains, on roads when walking.
Sometimes untidy, often elegant,
So easily hurt, so readily responsive,
To whom a trifle could be an irritant
Or could be balm and manna.
Whose words would tumble over each other and pelt
From pure excitement,
Whose fingers curl and melt
When you were friendly.
I shall remember you in bed with bright
Eyes or in a café stirring coffee
Abstractedly and on your plate the white
Smoking stub your lips had touched with crimson.
And I shall remember how your words could hurt
Because they were so honest
And even your lies were able to assert
Integrity of purpose.
And it is on the strength of knowing you
I reckon generous feeling more important
Than the mere deliberating what to do
When neither the pros nor cons affect the pulses.

And though I have suffered from your special strength
Who never flatter for points nor fake responses
I should be proud if I could evolve at length
An equal thrust and pattern.

MEETING POINT

Time was away and somewhere else,
There were two glasses and two chairs
And two people with the one pulse
(Somebody stopped the moving stairs):
Time was away and somewhere else.

And they were neither up nor down;
The stream's music did not stop
Flowing through heather, limpid brown,
Although they sat in a coffee shop
And they were neither up nor down.

The bell was silent in the air
Holding its inverted poise –
Between the clang and clang a flower,
A brazen calyx of no noise:
The bell was silent in the air.

The camels crossed the miles of sand
That stretched around the cups and plates;
The desert was their own, they planned
To portion out the stars and dates:
The camels crossed the miles of sand.

Time was away and somewhere else.
The waiter did not come, the clock
Forgot them and the radio waltz
Came out like water from a rock:
Time was away and somewhere else.

Her fingers flicked away the ash
That bloomed again in tropic trees:
Not caring if the markets crash
When they had forests such as these,
Her fingers flicked away the ash.

God or whatever means the Good
Be praised that time can stop like this,
That what the heart has understood
Can verify in the body's peace
God or whatever means the Good.

Time was away and she was here
And life no longer what it was,
The bell was silent in the air
And all the room one glow because
Time was away and she was here.

from NOVELETTES

II

LES SYLPHIDES

Life in a day: he took his girl to the ballet;
Being shortsighted himself could hardly see it –
The white skirts in the grey
Glade and the swell of the music
Lifting the white sails.

Calyx upon calyx, canterbury bells in the breeze
The flowers on the left mirror to the flowers on the right
And the naked arms above
The powdered faces moving
Like seaweed in a pool.

Now, he thought, we are floating – ageless, oarless –
Now there is no separation, from now on
You will be wearing white
Satin and a red sash
Under the waltzing trees.

But the music stopped, the dancers took their curtain,
The river had come to a lock – a shuffle of programmes –
And we cannot continue down
Stream unless we are ready
To enter the lock and drop.

So they were married – to be the more together –
And found they were never again so much together,
Divided by the morning tea
By the evening paper,
By children and tradesmen's bills.

Waking at times in the night she found assurance
Due to his regular breathing but wondered whether
It was really worth it and where
The river had flowed away
And where were the white flowers.

DÉJÀ VU

It does not come round in hundreds of thousands of years,
It comes round in the split of a wink, you will be sitting exactly
Where you are now and scratching your elbow, the train
Will be passing exactly as now and saying It does not come round,
It does not come round, It does not come round, and compactly
The wheels will mark time on the rails and the bird in the air
Sit tight in its box and the same bean of coffee be ground

That is now in the mill and I know what you're going to say
For all this has happened before, we both have been through
the mill,
Through our Magnus Annus, and now could all but call it a
day
Were it not that scratching your elbow you are too lovely by
half
So that, whatever the rules we might be supposed to obey,
Our love must extend beyond time because time is itself in
arrears
So this double vision must pass and past and future unite
And where we were told to kowtow we can snap our fingers
and laugh
And now, as you watch, I will take this selfsame pencil and
write:
It does not come round in hundreds of thousands of years.

THE INTRODUCTION

They were introduced in a grave glade
And she frightened him because she was young
And thus too late. Crawly crawly
Went the twigs above their heads and beneath
The grass beneath their feet the larvae
Split themselves laughing. Crawly crawly
Went the cloud above the treetops reaching
For a sun that lacked the nerve to set
And he frightened her because he was old
And thus too early. Crawly crawly
Went the string quartet that was tuning up
In the back of the mind. You two should have met
Long since, he said, or else not now.
The string quartet in the back of the mind
Was all tuned up with nowhere to go.
They were introduced in a green grave.

CODA

Maybe we knew each other better
When the night was young and unrepeated
And the moon stood still over Jericho.

So much for the past; in the present
There are moments caught between heart-beats
When maybe we know each other better.

But what is that clinking in the darkness?
Maybe we shall know each other better
When the tunnels meet beneath the mountain.

DENIS DEVLIN
1908–1959

from THE COLOURS OF LOVE

At the *Bar du Départ* drink farewell
And say no word you'll be remembered by;
Nor Prince nor President can ever tell
Where love ends or when it does or why.

Down the boulevard the lights come forth
Like my rainflowers trembling all through spring,
Blue and yellow in the Celtic North . . .
The stone's ripple weakens, ring by ring.

Better no love than love, which, through loving
Leads to no love. The ripples come to rest . . .
Ah me! how all that young year I was moving
To take her dissolution to my breast.

POEM

Waking in her arms of brightness
I feel as natural and safe
As children in their mother world.
The window brightens like a face
As morning opens the sea to the liners
And unparcels the cold towns.

Let me invent. I, day with eyes,
Am master of her, mere invert night;
Those eyelids dam the hundredweight
Sluices of light: she does not know:

And, conscious, I am king-priest
Of the mystery I have and watch.

Yet she is free, asleep and awake.
The bird's sharp note changes her face
Penetrating to her dream
Shut behind the impregnable
Petal walls of eyelids sweet,
Though I cup her face with fearful hands.

So precious that I realise
How it would be if she were not,
Because embossed upon extinction,
Burning and shining like the sun.
And from that black enemy, sleep,
May she emerge gold and shining!

W.R. RODGERS

1909–1969

THE LOVERS

After the tiff there was stiff silence, till
One word, flung in centre like single stone,
Starred and cracked the ice of her resentment
To its edge. From that stung core opened and
Poured up one outward and widening wave
Of eager and extravagant anger.

STORMY NIGHT

Is this the street? Never a sign of life,
The swinging lamp throws everything about;
But see! From that sly doorway, like a knife
The gilt edge of inviting light slides out
And in again – the very sign
Of her whose slightest nod I lately thought was mine;

But not now.
Knock! And the night-flowering lady
Opens, and across the brilliant sill
Sees me standing there so dark and shady
Hugging the silences of my ill-will;
Wildly she turns from me – But no, my love,
This foot's within the door, this hand's without the glove.

Well may you tremble now, and say there was nothing meant,
And curl away from my care with a 'Please, my dear!'
For though you were smoke, sucked up by a raging vent,
I'd follow you through every flue of your fear,
And over your faraway arms I'll mountain and cone
In a pillar of carolling fire and fountaining stone.

O strike the gong of your wrong, raise the roof of your rage,
Fist and foist me off with a cloud of cries,
What do I care for all your footling rampage?
On your light-in-gale blows my larking caresses will rise,
But – why so still? What! Are you weeping, my sweet?
Ah heart, heart, look! I throw myself at your feet.

LENT

Mary Magdalene, that easy woman,
Saw, from the shore, the seas
Beat against the hard stone of Lent,
Crying, 'Weep, seas, weep
For yourselves that cannot dent me more.

'O more than all these, more crabbed than all stones,
And cold, make me, who once
Could leap like water, Lord. Take me
As one who owes
Nothing to what she was. Ah, naked.

'My waves of scent, my petticoats of foam
Put from me and rebut;
Disown. And that salt lust stave off
That slavered me – O
Let it whiten in grief against the stones

'And outer reefs of me. Utterly doff,
Nor leave the lightest veil
Of feeling to heave or soften.
Nothing cares this heart
What hardness crates it now or coffins.

'Over the balconies of these curved breasts
I'll no more peep to see
The light procession of my loves

Surf-riding in to me
Who now have eyes and alcove, Lord, for Thee.'

'Room, Mary,' said He, 'ah make room for me
Who am come so cold now
To my tomb.' So, on Good Friday,
Under a frosty moon
They carried Him and laid Him in her womb.

A grave and icy mask her heart wore twice,
But on the third day it thawed,
And only a stone's-flow away
Mary saw her God.
Did you hear me? Mary saw her God!

Dance, Mary Magdalene, dance, dance and sing,
For unto you is born
This day a King. 'Lady,' said He,
'To you who relent
I bring back the petticoat and the bottle of scent.'

THE NET

Quick, woman, in your net
Catch the silver I fling!
O I am deep in your debt,
Draw tight, skin-tight, the string,
And rake the silver in.
No fisher ever yet
Drew such a cunning ring.

Ah, shifty as the fin
Of any fish this flesh
That, shaken to the shin,
Now shoals into your mesh,
Bursting to be held in;

Purse-proud and pebble-hard,
Its pence like shingle showered.

Open the haul, and shake
The fill of shillings free,
Let all the satchels break
And leap about the knee
In shoals of ecstasy.
Guineas and gills will flake
At each gull-plunge of me.

Though all the angels, and
Saint Michael at their head,
Nightly contrive to stand
On guard about your bed,
Yet none dare take a hand,
But each can only spread
His eagle-eye instead.

But I, being man, can kiss
And bed-spread-eagle too;
All flesh shall come to this,
Being less than angel is,
Yet higher far in bliss
As it entwines with you.

Come, make no sound, my sweet;
Turn down the candid lamp
And draw the equal quilt
Over our naked guilt.

WINTER'S COLD

May, and the wall was warm again. For miles
The welcoming air was lighted with smiles
Of homecoming hawthorn. Beat any bush

And a dust of birds flew out: lift a leaf,
There was laughter under. It was a day
For overtones and reveries of thunder.
Everyone walked in a haze, everything
Had a glory of stillness about it: hills
Had their hold-back of story. What shadow
Chilled our talk then? What high word screamed and was gone
Between us? Somewhere in air we heard it,
A stinging thong and rising weal of sound
Like a whoop and whip-round of bees swinging
Above the trees. She shivered, as if to say
'All the hives of our heart have swarmed today.'
Well, we hurriedly tried all sorts of things,
Drenched them in tears of protestation,
Ran everywhere, rooted out old buckets
Of good will, rattled odd tin-cans of kinship,
Looked up, of course, the book of usages,
But it was all no good: we could retract
Nothing. Silently
We watched the singing skein of our hopes
Unreel and roll across country
In the calm weather. Has anyone heard
Of them since? Is it, in a sense, only
The winter's cold that holds us together, lonely?

DONAGH MacDONAGH

1912–1968

PROTHALAMIUM

And so must I lose her whose mind
Fitted so sweetly and securely into mine
That words seeded and blossomed in an instant,
Whose body was one of my fine
Morning visions come alive and perfect?
Must she slip out of my arms so
And I never revel again in the twilight of her hair
Or see the world grow
Marvellous within her eye. My hands
Are empty; and suddenly I think
That on some night like this, when rain is soft
And moths flutter at the window, seeking a chink,
I'll lose her utterly, a bedded bride
Gold ring and contract bound,
The night filled with terrifying music
And she not hearing a sound.

BRÍDÍN VESEY

I would marry Brídín Vesey
Without a shoe or petticoat,
A comb, a cloak or dowry
Or even one clean shift;
And I would make novena
Or imitate the hermits
Who spend their lives in fasting
All for a Christmas gift.

O cheek like dogwood fruiting,
O cuckoo of the mountain,

I would send darkness packing
If you would rise and go
Against the ban of clergy
And the sour lips of your parents
And take me at an altar-stone
In spite of all Mayo.

That was the sullen morning
They told the cruel story,
How scorning word or token
You rose and went away.
'Twas then my hands remembered,
My ears still heard you calling,
I smelt the gorse and heather
Where you first learned to pray.
What could they know, who named you
Of jug and bed and table,
Hours slipping through our fingers,
Time banished from the room?
Or what of all the secrets
We knew among the rushes
Under the Reek when cuckoos
Brightened against the moon?

You are my first and last song,
The harp that lilts my fingers,
Your lips like frozen honey,
Eyes like the mountain pool,
Shaped like the Reek your breast is,
Whiter than milk from Nephin,
And he who never saw you
Has lived and died a fool.
Oh, gone across the mearing
Dividing hope from sadness
What happy townland holds you?
In what country do you reign?
In spite of all the grinning lads

At corner and in haybarn,
I'll search all Ireland over
And bring you home again.

AFTER THE IRISH (Anonymous, 17th–19th centuries)

PADRAIC FIACC

b. 1924

INTIMATE LETTER 1973

Our Paris part of Belfast has
Decapitated lamp-posts now. Our meeting
Place, the Book Shop, is a gaping
Black hole of charred timber.

Remember that night with you, in-
valided in the top room when
They were throwing petrol bombs through
The windows of Catholics, how
My migraine grew to such
A pitch, Brigid said 'Mommy,
I think Daddy is going to burst!'

We all run away from each other's
Particular hell. I didn't
Survive you and her thrown
To the floor when they blew up the Co-
Op at the bottom of the street or Brigid
Waking screaming after this
Or that explosion. Really,
I was the first one to go:

It was I who left you . . . .

DAVID MARCUS

b. 1924

from THE MIDNIGHT COURT

[A MAJESTIC MAID SPEAKS]

'The start of my story, the source of my strain,
The reason I'm senseless and almost insane,
The thing that has taken and torn me in twain
And has pricked me with pangs and has plagued me with pain –
Is the number of women, old and young,
For whom no wedding-bells have rung,
Who become in time mere hags and crones
Without man or money to warm their bones.
Thousands will back my evidence,
And I speak, alas, from experience;
Like me, I can swear, there's many another
Aching to be a wife and mother,
But the way we're ignored you'd think we're wrecks
Possessed of gender but not of sex;
At night with longing I'm lacerated,
Alone in bed I lie frustrated
And damned with dreams of desire denied
My hunger goes unsatisfied.
O Aeval, you must find a way
To save our women without delay,
For if the men are allowed to shirk
We'll have to force them to do their work.
By the time they're ready to take a wife
They're not worth taking to save their life,
They're stiff and shrunken and worn and weak
And when they mount you they wheeze and creak.
Then if, by chance, some lusty beau
Whose beard has hardly begun to grow
Decides to marry, whom does he wed –
Not a girl who is finely bred,

With fawn-like figure and fetching face,
Who knows how to carry herself with grace,
But a wicked witch or a female scrooge
Who gathered her dowry by subterfuge!'

[A WIZENED OLD JOSSER REPLIES]

'Aeval, listen to my report
And you'll throw that hussy out of court;
You'll pity the husbands of all these bitches
When I reveal who wears the breeches.
I was told by a pal – lives up the street –
As nice a lad as you'd ever meet,
A quiet, sober, decent man –
Until he married some harridan.
It galls me to see her on parade:
Such airs and graces as are displayed,
The way she boasts of her cows and crops
And opens accounts in the classiest shops.
I met her yesterday, face to face,
With her two fat breasts all over the place,
Swaying her hips like a ship in a storm
And generally running true to form;
Were it not for the fact that I'm discreet
And rather reluctant to repeat
The things I'm told, I could raise your hair
By recounting the times she's been stretched out bare,
On the flat of her back upon the ground
And the customers rushing from miles around.
From youth to grandad, all can speak
Of her adaptable technique –
In Ibrickane with big and small,
In Tirmaclane with one and all,
In Kilbrickane with thick and thin,
In Clare, in Ennis, and in Quin,
In Cratlee and Tradree where they're tough
She never seemed to have enough!

But I'd still have allowed her a second chance
And blamed it on youthful extravagance
Were it not that I saw with my own two eyes
On the roadway – naked to the skies –
Herself and a lout from the Durrus bogs
Going hammer and tongs like a couple of dogs.'

AFTER THE IRISH of Brian Merriman, 18th century

ANTHONY CRONIN

b. 1925

THE LOVER

All journeys end some place, and he was happy
Waiting for it to happen; there would be
Suddenly at a stop somebody laughing,
And looking from the window he would see

The scenery wheel into place composing
The proper setting and a mutual need
At evening would draw words and hands together
Until a love in doubt was love indeed.

But when he came where bands and tourists gathered
And she was there he found himself afraid,
And fumbled for that more successful other
And watched his personality recede

As in stepped once again the sad impostor
Who had stood in for him many times before,
The capable, the talkative, the clever,
Who thought his real self was such a bore

He would not even trust him in the moment
When the great clock of night shook warnings down
Of mornings which would come for every lover
When all but the sad daylight would be gone.

And through the days that followed he deceived her
About the waiting self behind his pride,
The self that stood there humbly, like a landscape,
Finding its plea for love again denied.

THE RISK

My love, since no lover yet
Approached the imagined good
But feared in his heart that he,
Dirty and scarred from the wood,

Might bring into that garden
(Where everything holds its peace
And the gardening sunlight never
Foresees the end of its lease)

All the litter of crime,
Old letters, the rags and bones
Which every clearing waits for
As a glasshouse waits for stones,

But from which perhaps in its silence
This green space might have been free
If he with a shout had not entered,
Tattered, anxious he;

And since my own disorders
The intimates I know,
Trail me as greedy familiars
Refusing daily to go;

And because the past we suffer
Can be contagious too
It seems odd to say I love you
And wish all this on you;

Except that like many another
Who glimpses the garden's grace
I cannot help also believing
That walking in that place

The spirit of the fountain
And the god of the bending tree
Might order a new beginning
And set one suddenly free

From the days that dog the daydream
When the heart turned to a stone
And the outcast stood there speechless
Forever now alone,

Because turning to me in the garden
You too who must face a day,
Illusory or real,
When a crime will come to stay,

Might with that shadow trembling
Beyond the garden wall
Declare that a human comfort
Is necessary after all.

FRANCIS HARVEY
b. 1925

AT ARDS

All day the pheasants were honking
like vintage cars and
the cows cropped
young grass with a sound of
rending cloth. The ferns
were uncurling their croziers under
the candelabra of the chestnuts and
the hills were blue, blue as
the pools of bluebells in the grass. There was
a smell of crushed
almonds in the airs eddying
from the whins and
you were there with
a flower in your hand and I
was with you and I wanted
to take your other hand but
the children were there
as well and the cows.
I knew they would stare.

SEÁN Ó TUAMA

b. 1926

SHE BEING 78, HE BEING 84

When they got married, we said
'They'll help to heat each other'
(she being 58, he being 64).
When he passed away we felt
bile rising in our mouths.

They had lived on dole and grants,
gossip their one solace –
but the dead face in the room now
was of an old king from the past.

She shrieked with rage, and combed him
with pagan fingerings
while we sound Christians prayed
that the lava-flow would stop.

She looked a widow of the Eastern world,
black shawl and moustached mouth,
the only woman in my lifetime
to have loved a prince
(she being 78, he being 84).

PATRICK GALVIN

b. 1927

THE NEGLECTED WIFE

Look, Woman
Go away from me.
I do not want you in my bed,
My feather bed with the four posters.
Besides, you are a married woman
With a poet for a husband
And I cannot renege
On a fellow-artist.

Don't tempt me.
It's true I've done it before –
My reputation haunts me.
But I was young then
And bloated with lechery.
Now my blood is like ice
And my mind is on holier things
Than a woman's genitals.

Laugh, if you will
But I'm tired of such nonsense.
Today, I can walk in the streets
With a fine conscience
Knowing I am safe from all harm
By demented husbands and distracted lovers.
The pleasures of old age
Are more than fabulous.

True, if I were young again
And flesh tormented
I might desire you greatly.
Your belly is rapturous as snow

And your bottom staggers me –
But that's by the way.
Control yourself now
And think how I've suffered.

I've had four husbands in my room
Shouting for my life
I've had lovers waiting on the stairs
To kick me on both shins.
No woman is worth such a sacrifice
And, besides, I no longer have the strength
Magnificent as you are
Lying there naked.

So remove yourself from my bed
And give my blessings to your husband –
But don't hurry yourself
Take time to dress.
And may Christ pardon me
This last fall.
It is an act of kindness
To a neglected wife.

Husbands and lovers
Do not condemn me
For the weakness in my loins
But pity me my lack of grace
And my poor upbringing
As God may pity you
In like circumstances.

PLAISIR D'AMOUR

SPRING

My father
Against the victories of age

Would not concede defeat,
He dyed his hair
And when my mother called
He said he wasn't there.

My mother, too
Fought back against the years
But in her Sunday prayers
Apologised to God.
My father said there was no God
'And that one knows it to her painted toes.'

My mother smiled.
She'd plucked her eyebrows too
And wore a see-through skirt
With matching vest.
'He likes French knickers best,' she said,
'I'll have them blest.'

My father raged.
He liked his women young, he said
And not half-dead.
He bought a second-hand guitar he couldn't play
And sang the only song he knew –
Plaisir d'amour.

SUMMER

When summer came
My father left the house.
He tied a ribbon in his hair
And wore a Kaftan dress.
My mother watched him walking down the street
'He'll break his neck in that,' she said –
'As if I care.'

He toured the world
And met a guru in Tibet.

'I've slept with women too,' he wrote,
'And they not half my age.'
My mother threw his letter in the fire –
'The lying ghett – he couldn't climb the stairs
With all his years.'

She burned her bra
And wrote with lipstick on a card –
'I've got two sailors in the house
From Martinique.
They've got your children's eyes.'
My father didn't wait to answer that –
He came back home.

And sitting by the fire
He said he'd lied
He'd never slept with anyone but her.
My mother said she'd never lied herself –
She'd thrown the sailors out an hour before he came.
My father's heart would never be the same –
Plaisir d'amour.

AUTUMN

Through autumn days
My father felt the leaves
Burning in the corners of his mind.

My mother, who was younger by a year,
Looked young and fair.
The sailors from the port of Martinique
Had kissed her cheek.

He searched the house
And hidden in a trunk beneath the bed
My father found his second-hand guitar.
He found her see-through skirt
With matching vest.

'You wore French knickers once,' he said,
'I liked them best.'

'I gave them all away,' my mother cried,
'To sailors and to captains of the sea.
I'm not half-dead
I'm fit for any bed – including yours.'
She wore a sailor's cap
And danced around the room
While father strummed his second-hand guitar.

He made the bed,
He wore his Kaftan dress,
A ribbon in his hair.
'I'll play it one more time,' he said,
'And you can sing.'
She sang the only song they knew –
Plaisir d'amour.

WINTER

At sixty-four
My mother died
At sixty-five
My father.

Comment from a neighbour
Who was there:
'They'd pass for twenty.'
Plaisir d'amour.

PEARSE HUTCHINSON

b. 1927

INTO THEIR TRUE GENTLENESS

for Katherine Kavanagh

If love is the greatest reality,
and I believe it is,
the gentle are more real
than the violent or than
those like me who
hate violence,
long for gentleness,
but never in our own act
achieve true gentleness.
We fall in love with people
we consider gentle,
we love them violently
for their gentleness,
so violently we drive
them to violence,
for our gentleness
is less real
than their breaking patience,
so falsely we accuse
them of being false.

But with any luck,
time half-opens our eyes
to at least a hundredth
part of our absurdity,
and lets them travel back,
released from us,
into their true gentleness,
even with us.

RICHARD KELL
b. 1927

SPRING NIGHT
for Muriel

Out on Killiney Hill that night, you said,
'Remember how we promised to come up here
when snow is lying under a full moon?'
And I made no reply – to hide my sadness,
thinking we might not satisfy that whim,
ever perhaps, at least for years to come,
since it was spring, and winter would see us parted.

Sitting on the Druid's Chair recalled
the last time we were there, a night of icy
wind and moonlight when the sea was churning
silver and the distant hills were clear;
how we belonged to them and they to us.
Now there was no brightness – only a vast
obscurity confusing sea and sky,
Dalkey Island and the lights of Bray
submerged and suffocating in the mist.

And there was no belonging now; no vivid
elemental statement to compel
refusal or assent, making decision
easy; but a dumb neutrality
that challenged us to give it character
and view our own minds large as a landscape.
To you it was tranquil. Sinister to me.

Lying under the pine tree, looking up
at the small stars and breathing the wood's sweetness,
we spoke hardly a word. I could not tell you

I was afraid of something out there
in the future, like that dark and bitter sea;
and how my love for you would have me lonely
until the fear was broken. I could say,
'Be close to me next winter and every winter;
we'll come up here to watch the snow by moonlight' –
and that would be too easy. For I must give
to you whose meaning transcends moods and moments
nothing half-hearted or ambiguous,
but the perfected diamond of my will.

from HEARTWOOD

MARRIAGE IS LIKE A TREE

After the flood, its roots are dying in air.
When twenty-two rings of tough growth
fell in a race of water,
the bark was lumpy with healed wounds,
the heartwood sound.

I recall, with a love that's inward now,
its many changes: foliage playing
in light, drooping in damp glooms
or stilled by rich calms of summer;
branches furred with snow, or their stormy thrashing.

How sad, these emptied places. But elsewhere
you find, again with sadness, trees that were hurt
too deeply, unnerved by pest and fungus,
hollowing to their last stand
against the rising wind.

It could be a kind of luck, being left
the ghost of a scarred tree

still healthy when it toppled:
leaves whispering through all the mind's seasons,
a root safe in the ground for ever.

FOR THE YOUNG PEOPLE

My sons and daughters, what could I say to you
in a vast emptiness, that wouldn't sound
remote or insufficient or untrue
compared with the simple statement 'She was drowned'?
Yet, in an age when interstellar night
dissolves the Cross, the Ark, and Moses' rod,
I could still wonder whether it was right
not to have taught you to believe in God.

Finally, all I said was 'Try to be
as she'd have wished you – as you've always been.'
Sharing the work, concerned for one another,
learning to hope again, and helping me
to do the same, you span the void between
a mythic father and a real mother.

RICHARD MURPHY

b. 1927

SEALS AT HIGH ISLAND

The calamity of seals begins with jaws.
Born in caverns that reverberate
With endless malice of the sea's tongue
Clacking on shingle, they learn to bark back
In fear and sadness and celebration.
The ocean's mouth opens forty feet wide
And closes on a morsel of their rock.

Swayed by the thrust and backfall of the tide,
A dappled grey bull and a brindled cow
Copulate in the green water of a cove.
I watch from a cliff-top, trying not to move.
Sometimes they sink and merge into black shoals;
Then rise for air, his muzzle on her neck,
Their winged feet intertwined as a fishtail.

She opens her fierce mouth like a scarlet flower
Full of white seeds; she holds it open long
At the sunburst in the music of their loving;
And cries a little. But I must remember
How far their feelings are from mine marooned.
If there are tears at this holy ceremony
Theirs are caused by brine and mine by breeze.

When the great bull withdraws his rod, it glows
Like a carnelian candle set in jade.
The cow ripples ashore to feed her calf;
While an old rival, eyeing the deed with hate,
Swims to attack the tired triumphant god.
They rear their heads above the boiling surf,
Their terrible jaws open, jetting blood.

At nightfall they haul out, and mourn the drowned,
Playing to the sea sadly their last quartet,
An improvised requiem that ravishes
Reason, while ripping scale up like a net:
Brings pity trembling down the rocky spine
Of headlands, till the bitter ocean's tongue
Swells in their cove, and smothers their sweet song.

SUNUP

The sun kisses my eyes open:
Another day of wanting you.
I'd like to kiss your eyes again,
No comfort now in being alone.

Is she delighting you in bed
In her caravan on a cutaway road?
Does the sun give you the same kiss
To wake you, with her at your side?

I kiss you both, like the sun,
I kiss your hands and your feet,
Your ears and your eyes,
Both your bodies, I bless them both.

Do you feel this when you make love?
Do you love her as I loved you?
Will you let her steal all you have
And suffer her to leave?

Meet me today! We'll find a wood
Of blackthorn in white bud:
And let me give you one more kiss
Full of sun, free of bitterness.

MOONSHINE

To think
I must be alone:
To love
We must be together.

I think I love you
When I'm alone
More than I think of you
When we're together.

I cannot think
Without loving
Or love
Without thinking.

Alone I love
To think of us together:
Together I think
I'd love to be alone.

A NEST IN A WALL

Smoky as peat your lank hair on my pillow
Burns like a tinker's fire in a mossy ditch.
Before I suffocate, let me slowly suck
From your mouth a tincture of mountain ash,
A red infusion of summer going to seed.
Ivy clumps loosen the stonework of my heart.
Come like a wood pigeon gliding there to roost!

I float a moment on a gust sighing for ever
Gently over your face where two swans swim.
Let me kiss your eyes in the slate-blue calm
Before their Connemara clouds return.

A spancelled goat bleats in our pleasure ground.
A whippet snarls on its chain. The fire dies out.
Litter of rags and bottles in the normal rain.

Your country and mine, love, can it still exist?
The unsignposted hawthorn lane of your body
Leads to my lichenous walls and gutted house.
Your kind of beauty earth has almost lost.
Although we have no home in the time that's come,
Coming together we live in our own time.
Make your nest of moss like a wren in my skull.

DISPLACED PERSON

Those years ago, when I made love to you,
    With fears I was afraid you knew,
    To grow strong I'd pretend to be
A boy I'd loved, loving yourself as me.
I played his part so open-eyed that you
    Believed my artful ploy was true.
    To show I'd nothing false to hide
And make you feel the truth of love I lied.

The love of truth made me confess, and died
    Exposing my hermetic guide,
    A youth found loitering in the mart
Of memory's torn-down inner-city heart.
I feel betrayed by dead words that decide
    If head or tail be certified.
    Dear girl, come back and take a new
Lover in me, let him make love to you.

THOMAS KINSELLA

b. 1928

A LADY OF QUALITY

In hospital where windows meet
With sunlight in a pleasing feat
    Of airy architecture
My love has sweets and grapes to eat,
The air is like a laundered sheet,
    The world's a varnished picture.

Books and flowers at her head
Make living quarters of her bed
    And give a certain style
To our pillow-chat, the nonsense said
To bless the room from present dread
    Just for a brittle while.

For obvious reasons we ignore
The leaping season out-of-door,
    Light lively as a ferret,
Woodland walks, a crocused shore,
The transcendental birds that soar
    And tumble in high spirit

While under this hygienic ceiling
Where my love lies down for healing
    Tiny terrors grow,
Reflected in a look, revealing
That her care is spent concealing
    What, perhaps, I know:

The ever-present crack in time
Forever sundering the lime-
    Paths and the fragrant fountains,

Photographed last summer, from
The unknown memory we climb
        To find in this year's mountains.

'Ended and done with' never ceases,
Constantly the heart releases
        Wild geese to the past.
Look, how they circle poignant places,
Falling to sorrow's fowling-pieces
        With soft plumage aghast.

We may regret, and must abide.
Grief, the hunter's, fatal stride
        Among the darkening hearts
Has gone too long on either side.
Our trophied love must now divide
        Into its separate parts

And you go down with womankind
Who in her beauty has combined
        And focused human hungers,
With country ladies who could wind
A nation's love-affair with mind
        Around their little fingers,

And I communicate again
Recovered order to my pen
        To find a further answer
As, having looked all night in vain,
A weary prince will sigh and then
        Take a familiar dancer.

Now the window's turning dark
And ragged rooks across the Park
        Mix with the branches; all
The clocks about the building mark

The hour. The random is at work
        On us: two petals fall,

A train lifts up a lonely cry . . .
Our fingertips together lie
        Upon the counterpane.
It will be hard, it seems, and I
Would wish my heart to justify
        What qualities remain.

—

CHRYSALIDES

Our last free summer we mooned about at odd hours
Pedalling slowly through country towns, stopping to eat
Chocolate and fruit, tracing our vagaries on the map.

At night we watched in the barn, to the lurch of melodeon music,
The crunching boots of countrymen – huge and weightless
As their shadows – twirling and leaping over the yellow concrete.

Sleeping too little or too much, we awoke at noon
And were received with womanly mockery into the kitchen,
Like calves poking our faces in with enormous hunger.

Daily we strapped our saddlebags and went to experience
A tolerance we shall never know again, confusing
For the last time, for example, the licit and the familiar.

Our instincts blurred with change; a strange wakefulness
Sapped our energies and dulled our slow-beating hearts
To the extremes of feeling – insensitive alike

To the unique succession of our youthful midnights,
When by a window ablaze softly with the virgin moon
Dry scones and jugs of milk awaited us in the dark,

Or to lasting horror: a wedding flight of ants
Spawning to its death, a mute perspiration
Glistening like drops of copper in our path.

FIRST LIGHT

A prone couple still sleeps.
Light ascends like a pale gas
Out of the sea: dawn-
Light, reaching across the hill
To the dark garden. The grass
Emerges, soaking with grey dew.

Inside, in silence, an empty
Kitchen takes form, tidied and swept,
Blank with marriage – where shrill
Lover and beloved have kept
Another vigil far
Into the night, and raved and wept.

Upstairs a whimper or sigh
Comes from an open bedroom door
And lengthens to an ugly wail
– A child enduring a dream
That grows, at the first touch of day,
Unendurable.

JOHN MONTAGUE
b. 1929

ALL LEGENDARY OBSTACLES

All legendary obstacles lay between
Us, the long imaginary plain,
The monstrous ruck of mountains
And, swinging across the night,
Flooding the Sacramento, San Joaquin,
The hissing drift of winter rain.

All day I waited, shifting
Nervously from station to bar
As I saw another train sail
By, the San Francisco Chief or
Golden Gate, water dripping
From great flanged wheels.

At midnight you came, pale
Above the negro porter's lamp.
I was too blind with rain
And doubt to speak, but
Reached from the platform
Until our chilled hands met.

You had been travelling for days
With an old lady, who marked
A neat circle on the glass
With her glove, to watch us
Move into the wet darkness
Kissing, still unable to speak.

THAT ROOM

Side by side on the narrow bed
We lay, like chained giants,
Tasting each other's tears, in terror
Of the news which left little to hide
But our two faces that stared
To ritual masks, absurd and flayed.

Rarely in a lifetime comes such news
Shafting knowledge straight to the heart
Making shameless sorrow start –
Not childish tears, querulously vain –
But adult tears that hurt and harm,
Seeping like acid to the bone.

Sound of hooves on the midnight road
Raised a dramatic image to mind:
The Dean riding late to Marley?
But we must suffer the facts of self;
No one endures a similar fate
And no one will ever know

What happened in that room
But when we came to leave
We scrubbed each other's tears,
Prepared the usual show. That day
Love's claims made chains of time and place
To bind us together more: equal in adversity.

UPROOTING

My love, while we talked
They removed the roof. Then
They started on the walls,
Panes of glass uprooting

From timber, like teeth.
But you spoke calmly on,
Your example of courtesy
Compelling me to reply.
When we reached the last
Syllable, nearly accepting
Our positions, I saw that
The floorboards were gone:
It was clay we stood upon.

THE SAME GESTURE

There is a secret room
of golden light where
everything – love, violence,
hatred is possible;
and, again, love.

Such intimacy of hand
and mind is achieved
under its healing light
that the shifting of
hands is a rite

like court music.
We barely know our
selves there though
it is what we always were
– most nakedly are –

and must remember
when we leave, re-
suming our habits
with our clothes:
work, phone, drive

through late traffic
changing gears with
the same gesture as
eased your snowbound
heart and flesh.

LOVE, A GREETING

Love, a greeting
in the night, a
passing kindness,
wet leaf smell
of hair, skin

or a lifetime's
struggle to exchange
with the strange
thing inhabiting
a woman –
face,
breasts, buttocks,
the honey sac
of the cunt –

luring us to forget,
beget, a form of truth
or (the last rhyme
tolls its half tone)
an answer to death.

TRACKS

I

The vast bedroom
a hall of air,

our linked bodies
lying there.

II

As I turn to kiss
your long, black
hair, small breasts,
heat flares from
your fragrant skin,
your eyes widen as
deeper, more certain
and often, I enter
to search possession
of where your being
hides in flesh.

III

Behind our eyelids
a landscape opens,
a violet horizon
pilgrims labour across,
a sky of colours
that change, explode
a fantail of stars
the mental lightning
of sex illuminating
the walls of the skull;
a floating pleasure dome.

IV

I shall miss you
creaks the mirror
into which the scene
shortly disappears:
the vast bedroom
a hall of air, the

tracks of our bodies
fading there, while
giggling maids push
a trolley of fresh
linen down the corridor.

SHE WALKS ALONE

In the white city of Evora, absence accosted me.
You were reading in bed, while I walked all night alone.
Were you worried about me, or drifting towards sleep?

I saw the temple of Diana, bone-white in the moonlight.
I made a private prayer to her, for strength to continue:
Not since convent days have I prayed so earnestly.

A dog came out of the shadows, brushed against my leg.
He followed me everywhere, pushing his nose into my hand.
Soon the cats appeared, little scraggy bundles of need.

There were more monuments, vivid as hallucinations.
Suddenly, a young man stepped out of the shadows:
I was not terrified, as I might have been at home.

Besides, he was smiling and gentle as you used to be.
'A kiss,' he pleads, 'a kiss,' in soft Portuguese.
I quickened my step, but he padded behind me.

He looked so young, my heart went out to him.
I stopped in the shadows under the Cathedral.
We kissed, and the tears poured down my face.

HERBERT STREET REVISITED

for Madeleine

I

A light is burning late
in this Georgian Dublin street:
someone is leading our old lives!

And our black cat scampers again
through the wet grass of the convent garden
upon his masculine errands.

The pubs shut: a released bull,
Behan shoulders up the street,
topples into our basement, roaring 'John!'

A pony and donkey cropped flank
by flank under the trees opposite;
short neck up, long neck down,

as Nurse Mullen knelt by her bedside
to pray for her lost Mayo hills,
the bruised bodies of Easter Volunteers.

Animals, neighbours, treading the pattern
of one time and place into history,
like our early marriage, while

tall windows looked down upon us
from walls flushed light pink or salmon
watching and enduring succession.

II

As I leave, you whisper,
'don't betray our truth'
and like a ghost dancer,

invoking a lost tribal strength
I halt in tree-fed darkness

to summon back our past,
and celebrate a love that eased
so kindly, the dying bone,
enabling the spirit to sing
of old happiness, when alone.

III

So put the leaves back on the tree,
put the tree back in the ground,
let Brendan trundle his corpse down
the street singing, like Molly Malone.

Let the black cat, tiny emissary
of our happiness, streak again
through the darkness, to fall soft
clawed into a landlord's dustbin.

Let Nurse Mullen take the last
train to Westport, and die upright
in her chair, facing a window
warm with the blue slopes of Nephin.

And let the pony and donkey come –
look, someone has left the gate open –
like hobbyhorses linked in
the slow motion of a dream

parading side by side, down
the length of Herbert Street,
rising and falling, lifting
their hooves through the moonlight.

EDGE

Edenlike as your name
this sea's edge garden
where we rest, beneath
the clarity of a lighthouse.

To fly into risk,
attempt the dream,
cast off, as we have done,
requires true luck

who know ourselves
blessed to have found
between this harbour's arms
a sheltering home

where the vast
tides of the Atlantic
lift to caress
rose coloured rocks.

So fate relents.
Hushed and calm,
safe and secret,
on the edge is best.

TOM MacINTYRE
b. 1933

SWEET KILLEN HILL

Flower of the flock,
Any time, any land,
Plenty your ringlets,
Plenty your hand,
Sunlight your window,
Laughter your sill,
And I must be with you
On sweet Killen Hill.

Let sleep renege me,
Skin lap my bones,
Love and tomorrow
Can handle the reins,
You my companion
I'd never breathe ill,
And I guarantee bounty
On sweet Killen Hill.

You'll hear the pack yell
As puss devil-dances,
Hear cuckoo and thrush
Pluck song from the branches,
See fish in the pool
Doing their thing,
And the bay as God made it
From sweet Killen Hill.

Pulse of my life,
We come back to – *mise,*
Why slave for McArdle –

That bumbailiff's issue,
I've a harp in a thousand,
Love songs at will,
And the air is cadenza
On sweet Killen Hill.

Gentle one, lovely one,
Come to me,
Now sleep the clergy,
Now sleep their care,
Sunrise will find us
But sunrise won't tell
That Love lacks surveillance
On sweet Killen Hill.

AFTER THE IRISH of Peadar Ó Doirnín, 18th century

CATHLEEN

Lovely whore though,
Lovely, lovely whore,
And choosy –
Slept with Conn,
Slept with Niall,
Slept with Brian,
Slept with Rory.

Slide then,
The long slide.

Of course it shows.

AFTER THE IRISH of Owen Roe O'Sullivan, 18th century

JAMES SIMMONS
b. 1933

BALLAD OF A MARRIAGE

'This sweet, mysterious country
explored by my right hand.
Am I the first, my wife, that's burst
into this silent land?'
She said she hadn't been a whore,
but she had lain with men before.

I'd slept with girls myself, but I
was trembling, I was hating
these men, and her, and yet I found
her stories titillating:
first fascination, then disgust;
first pain, and then a surge of lust.

Playing with words as children play
with toys had been a thrill,
but now the cuddly lion had jaws,
the little gun could kill.
Freedom and Truth, by which I swear,
in fact were more than I could bear.

When she stirred under me I saw her
squirming in delight
in other people's cars and beds,
and sitting up all night,
her face drained white in love's despair
because some man had not been there.

To freeze the pain of this I froze
my love. I read much more
and thought alone and talked to friends

till 3 a.m. and 4.
And came to bed the worse for beer,
and was annoyed to have her near.

She cried a lot and fought, surprised;
knowing love she felt the lack.
Love? What was love? I only felt
her dead weight on my back.
We stayed together out of shame
and habit, and then children came.

But books and thought and talk aren't drugs,
they query and accuse:
where do you hope to go from here?
What are you going to lose?
And just to fight and tell her lies
I had to look and see her eyes.

As green shoots push through hardened soil
where nothing seemed to be,
so tenderness, caresses, jokes
grew out of her and me.
No families wave, no organs play,
this long and gradual wedding day.

HUSBAND TO WIFE

When I consider how your life was spent
before we met, I see a parked car
where some man took you, dear, with your consent,
and helped to make you what you are.
From both of you there is the smell of beer;
I feel you thrilled at last to be alone,
not missing me – well, how could I be there! –
exploring him and being explored and known.
My fancy pushes towards pornography

the necessary sweet acts of lust.
Then you undid his flies, unblushingly,
with cool hands, then a joke, a smile of trust,
then took his weight and smelt and felt his breath,
then held and guided underneath your skin
his rosy, swelling penis, in a sheath,
filling you up as it came in,
just as mine does, my bride,
just as mine does. Such thoughts have made me sweat
and wrestle hours, no, years, against my pride;
and, to be honest, I am wrestling yet.
You are because you were, and when I love
I love because and not in spite of this,
and you, not waiting till I rise above,
cleave to uneasiness.

I'LL NEVER SAY GOODBYE

At the end of the Serpentine,
Lancaster Gate,
on a morning last January,
having to wait,
I walked where I used to walk
fifteen years gone
by the elegant, worn-away
fountains of stone.

Like a stone-shattered windscreen
the water rose white
against air on the left
and black trees on the right.
With small swans beside them,
in stone, at their ease,
were two big girls holding
their ewers on their knees.

Exactly your features,
the strength of your back,
the curve of your breasts
and the chin that you lack.
Your body a fountain
with life thrusting out,
and this must be the sister
you told me about.

This is my part of London.
I'm happy to know
that your statue looks down
where I once used to row,
and whenever I pass here
on poetry tours,
by the Serpentine fountains
my time will be yours.

THE SILENT MARRIAGE

A song

With your clothes on the chair
and one white sheet above you
I have no need of words
to explain how I love you.
Every touch of delight
through the long wedding night
is defining our love.
With this kiss I thee wed.

If our luck should run out
and love withers and dies, love,
don't try out of kindness
to save me with lies, love.
You won't need to explain
that I'm single again

and the marriage is done
when your kiss says goodbye.

from MARITAL SONNETS

1

She was brought up like most girls of that age
to rouse lust in the casual passer-by.
Tight skirts and nylons and décolletage
stirred lust she wasn't taught to satisfy.
Her nerve and frankness made her seem a flirt
when all she really wanted was a friend.
Men talked until their hands were up her skirt:
she got it over, but it was the end.
Some, looking back, could sense that they had missed
something for which they hadn't been prepared.
They told their troubles to her and got pissed
and left. At twenty she was tired and scared,
bitter and frigid and without resource,
but still *the hottest thing in town,* of course.

2

When I was twenty-four I was so lonely
I married her to keep me company
and learned to value solitude the hard way.
It turned out that a husband must have money.
I fastened on the old chains I had broken,
I took direction and prepared to sit
exams, made notes on rubbish spoken
by cultivated hacks, was paid for it.
My joy in reading atrophied.
Hatred and guilt and laziness
increased. In drink I sneered or cried,
vomited up and ate my own mess,
and in due course had limited success
constructing poems from unhappiness.

GOODBYE, SALLY

Shaken already, I know
I'll wake at night after you go
watching the soft shine of your skin,
feeling your little buttocks, oh my grief,
like two duck eggs in a handkerchief,
barely a woman but taking me all in.

I think our love won't die –
but there I go trying to justify!
What odds that we'll never meet again
and probably other girls will never
bring half your agony of pleasure?
Fidelity is a dumb pain.

God, but I'm lucky too,
the way I've muddled through
to ecstasy so often despite
exhaustion, drunkenness and pride.
How come that you were satisfied
and so was I that night?

It's true for drinker and lover,
the best stuff has no hangover.
You're right to spit on argument,
girl. Your dumbness on a walk
was better than my clown's talk.
You showed me what you meant.

Good mornings from every night
with you, thirsty and sore with appetite.
You never let me act my age.
Goodbye to all analysis and cause-
grubbing. The singer wants applause
not criticism as he leaves the stage.

FOR IMELDA

There were no poems that year,
but every night driving from work
the red haws on the hedges
took me unawares, looming
in the milky car beams
as lush as cherries;
a sign they said of the hard
winter to come or maybe
the loveliest summer
in living memory,
my memory, my dear.

AFTER EDEN

His last glimpse of the former wife
is after midnight, woozy with drink,
on a quick foray for old tapes,
and the front door is open, as always,
out of their shared instinct.

A ghost in his own shadowy hall,
the stairwell echoing still
with bitter shouting and slammed doors,
up in his old study he opens drawers,
and descends, his thieving arms full.

A man comes out of the kitchen and disappears.
At the car the wife grabs him, hissing abuse.
Hunched awkwardly, unloading his loot,
his high-pitched voice whining, 'Christ,
you've got everything else!' – he breaks loose,

'Look, we agreed . . .' 'I agreed to nothing!
It was *you* walked out on *me* with your whore!'

When he hits her, precious tapes unreel
and roll on the pavement. Again they are sharing
intimate touch – her nose, his knuckles, sore.

Will the long marriage never be over?
Love she would call what drives her now to close
fiercely against him, drinking his anger,
shameless and righteous, fronting
her husband, embracing his futile blows.

His last glimpse is of her standing
in faded chiffon nightwear, humble, beautiful,
like a dark harvest etching, *The Last Gleaner,*
a woman, lit by a street lamp, winding
tangles of gleaming tape on a plastic spool.

THE HONEYMOON

Remember last summer when God turned on the heat
and browned our bodies, remember how hard and sweet
were the green apples you bought.
Remember how quickly neglected nipples were taught
to take pleasure in kissing. Remember your sunburn peeled
after a day on the grass of the hill field
and the painless scars evoked a principle for us,
that the truly lovely is truly ridiculous.

A beauty like you can look sometimes dumpy and fat,
knock-kneed, hen-toed, and none the worse for that,
for when you recover your splendour suddenly
what seemed like flaws is personality.
The world has examined you closely and found you right
and beautiful with a more piercing sight
than fashion editors know. You thought I meant
evasion, a left-handed compliment,
but now know better, being able to talk to you
like this is love being true.

Nothing could get us down those days together
but lust, on grass, in mountain streams when the weather
was hot as ourselves, on collapsing sofas, on floors,
in the steamed-up Datsun in the great outdoors.
Our best man swore you would be black and blue,
and, true enough, love's frightening. You do
violent-seeming things; but no one's hurt,
playing by the rules. We rise from dirt,
stink, struggle, shining, having suffered nothing.
No wonder they say that God would have us loving.

The worst débâcle was, once, trying to screw,
erect, me knees-bent, on my feet, and you
tiptoe on Dickens's *Our Mutual Friend*.
No joy. Abashed, we thought it was the end
of something; but no, failing is all right,
a sort of roughage to the appetite.

Our strangest luck seemed, first, not good, but ill –
me slow to come, you inexhaustible.
That turned out well. I had not thought God's voice
was intricate and humorous, like Joyce's.

Even your tears, after our first quarrel
when you got strangely thick and I got moral,
was not exploitive. Remember our briny kiss?
Nothing was broken, nothing was amiss.

DESMOND O'GRADY

b. 1935

THE POET LOVES FROM HIS DISTANCE

I think now I'll whore it up for a while
and quit making out to be what I'm not.
Women with balls who'd cramp any man's style
make a dangerous lot.

Although it's women of wholesome structure
men on the make most want to bed,
there's a girl called Gormflah I'd like to fracture
and no word said.

If I had the pick of the ripest locals,
the hottest from here to the town of Maynooth,
a hammer at her would loosen my yokles,
stretched or stood up.

AFTER THE IRISH (Anonymous, 16th–17th centuries)

BRENDAN KENNELLY

b. 1936

BREAD

Someone else cut off my head
In a golden field.
Now I am re-created

By her fingers. This
Moulding is more delicate
Than a first kiss,

More deliberate than her own
Rising up
And lying down.

Even at my weakest, I am
Finer than anything
In this legendary garden

Yet I am nothing till
She runs her fingers through me
And shapes me with her skill.

The form that I shall bear
Grows round and white.
It seems I comfort her

Even as she slits my face
And stabs my chest.
Her feeling for perfection is

Absolute.
So I am glad to go through fire
And come out

Shaped like her dream.
In my way
I am all that can happen to men.
I came to life at her fingerends.
I will go back into her again.

WE ARE LIVING

What is this room
But the moments we have lived in it?
When all due has been paid
To gods of wood and stone
And recognition has been made
Of those who breathe here when we are gone,
Does it not take its worth from us
Who made it because we were here?

Your words are the only furniture I can remember,
Your body the book that told me most.
If this room has a ghost
It will be your laughter in the frank dark,
Revealing the world as a room
Loved only for those moments when
We touched the purely human.

I could give water now to thirsty plants,
Dig up the floorboards, the foundation,
Study the worm's confidence,
Challenge his omnipotence
Because my blind eyes have seen through walls
That make safe prisons of the days.

We are living
In ceiling, floor and windows,
We are given to where we have been.

This white door will always open
On what our hands have touched,
Our eyes have seen.

SEAMUS HEANEY

b. 1939

SUMMER HOME

I

Was it wind off the dumps
or something in heat

dogging us, the summer gone sour,
a fouled nest incubating somewhere?

Whose fault, I wondered, inquisitor
of the possessed air.

To realise suddenly,
whip off the mat

that was larval, moving –
and scald, scald, scald.

II

Bushing the door, my arms full
of wild cherry and rhododendron,
I hear her small lost weeping
through the hall, that bells and hoarsens
on my name, my name.

O love, here is the blame.

The loosened flowers between us
gather in, compose
for a May altar of sorts.
These frank and falling blooms
soon taint to a sweet chrism.

Attend. Anoint the wound.

III

O we tented our wound all right
under the homely sheet

and lay as if the cold flat of a blade
had winded us.

More and more I postulate
thick healings, like now

as you bend in the shower
water lives down the tilting stoups of your breasts.

IV

With a final
unmusical drive
long grains begin
to open and split

ahead and once more
we sap
the white, trodden
path to the heart.

V

My children weep out the hot foreign night.
We walk the floor, my foul mouth takes it out
On you and we lie stiff till dawn
Attends the pillow, and the maize, and vine

That holds its filling burden to the light.
Yesterday rocks sang when we tapped
Stalactites in the cave's old, dripping dark –
Our love calls tiny as a tuning fork.

from GLANMORE SONNETS

X

I dreamt we slept in a moss in Donegal
On turf banks under blankets, with our faces
Exposed all night in a wetting drizzle,
Pallid as the dripping sapling birches.
Lorenzo and Jessica in a cold climate.
Diarmuid and Grainne waiting to be found.
Darkly asperged and censed, we were laid out
Like breathing effigies on a raised ground.
And in that dream I dreamt – how like you this? –
Our first night years ago in that hotel
When you came with your deliberate kiss
To raise us towards the lovely and painful
Covenants of flesh; our separateness;
The respite in our dewy dreaming faces.

THE OTTER

When you plunged
The light of Tuscany wavered
And swung through the pool
From top to bottom.

I loved your wet head and smashing crawl,
Your fine swimmer's back and shoulders
Surfacing and surfacing again
This year and every year since.

I sat dry-throated on the warm stones.
You were beyond me.
The mellowed clarities, the grape-deep air
Thinned and disappointed.

Thank God for the slow loadening,

When I hold you now
We are close and deep
As the atmosphere on water.

My two hands are plumbed water.
You are my palpable, lithe
Otter of memory
In the pool of the moment,

Turning to swim on your back,
Each silent, thigh-shaking kick
Re-tilting the light
Heaving the cool at your neck.

And suddenly you're out,
Back again, intent as ever,
Heavy and frisky in your freshened pelt,
Printing the stones.

THE SKUNK

Up, black, striped and damasked like the chasuble
At a funeral mass, the skunk's tail
Paraded the skunk. Night after night
I expected her like a visitor.

The refrigerator whinnied into silence.
My desk light softened beyond the verandah.
Small oranges loomed in the orange tree.
I began to be tense as a voyeur.

After eleven years I was composing
Love-letters again, broaching the word 'wife'
Like a stored cask, as if its slender vowel
Had mutated into the night earth and air

Of California. The beautiful, useless
Tang of eucalyptus spelt your absence.
The aftermath of a mouthful of wine
Was like inhaling you off a cold pillow.

And there she was, the intent and glamorous,
Ordinary, mysterious skunk,
Mythologised, demythologised,
Snuffing the boards five feet beyond me.

It all came back to me last night, stirred
By the sootfall of your things at bedtime,
Your head-down, tail-up hunt in a bottom drawer
For the black plunge-line nightdress.

A DREAM OF JEALOUSY

Walking with you and another lady
In wooded parkland, the whispering grass
Ran its fingers through our guessing silence
And the trees opened into a shady
Unexpected clearing where we sat down.
I think the candour of the light dismayed us.
We talked about desire and being jealous,
Our conversation a loose single gown
Or a white picnic tablecloth spread out
Like a book of manners in the wilderness.
'Show me,' I said to our companion, 'what
I have much coveted, your breast's mauve star.'
And she consented. O neither these verses
Nor my prudence, love, can heal your wounded stare.

from FIELD WORK

IV

Catspiss smell,
the pink bloom open:
I press a leaf
of the flowering currant
on the back of your hand
for the tight slow burn
of its sticky juice
to prime your skin,
and your veins to be crossed
criss-cross with leaf-veins.
I lick my thumb
and dip it in mould,
I anoint the anointed
leaf-shape. Mould
blooms and pigments
the back of your hand
like a birthmark –
my umber one,
you are stained, stained
to perfection.

THE UNDERGROUND

There we were in the vaulted tunnel running,
You in your going-away coat speeding ahead
And me, me then like a fleet god gaining
Upon you before you turned to a reed

Or some new white flower japped with crimson
As the coat flapped wild and button after button
Sprang off and fell in a trail
Between the Underground and the Albert Hall.

Honeymooning, moonlighting, late for the Proms,
Our echoes die in that corridor and now
I come as Hansel came on the moonlit stones
Retracing the path back, lifting the buttons

To end up in a draughty lamplit station
After the trains have gone, the wet track
Bared and tensed as I am, all attention
For your step following and damned if I look back.

SLOE GIN

The clear weather of juniper
darkened into winter.
She fed gin to sloes
and sealed the glass container.

When I unscrewed it
I smelled the disturbed
tart stillness of a bush
rising through the pantry.

When I poured it
it had a cutting edge
and flamed
like Betelgeuse.

I drink to you
in smoke-mirled, blue-black,
polished sloes, bitter
and dependable.

from CLEARANCES

7

In the last minutes he said more to her
Almost than in all their life together.
'You'll be in New Row on Monday night
And I'll come up for you and you'll be glad
When I walk in the door . . . Isn't that right?'
His head was bent down to her propped-up head.
She could not hear but we were overjoyed.
He called her good and girl. Then she was dead,
The searching for a pulsebeat was abandoned
And we all knew one thing by being there.
The space we stood around had been emptied
Into us to keep, it penetrated
Clearances that suddenly stood open.
High cries were felled and a pure change happened.

MICHAEL LONGLEY

b. 1939

EPITHALAMION

  These are the small hours when
Moths by their fatal appetite
That brings them tapping to get in,
  Are steered along the night
To where our window catches light.

  Who hazard all to be
Where we, the only two it seems,
Inhabit so delightfully
  A room it bursts its seams
And spills on to the lawn in beams,

  Such visitors as these
Reflect with eyes like frantic stars
This garden's brightest properties,
  Cruising its corridors
Of light above the folded flowers,

  Till our vicinity
Is rendered royal by their flight
Towards us, till more silently
  The silent stars ignite,
Their aeons dwindling by a night,

  And everything seems bent
On robing in this evening you
And me, all dark the element
  Our light is earnest to,
All quiet gathered round us who,

When over the embankments
A train that's loudly reprobate
Shoots from silence into silence,
With ease accommodate
Its pandemonium, its freight.

I hold you close because
We have decided dark will be
For ever like this and because,
My love, already
The dark is growing elderly.

With dawn upon its way,
Punctually and as a rule,
The small hours widening into day
Our room its vestibule
Before it fills all houses full,

We too must hazard all,
Switch off the lamp without a word
For the last of night assembled
Over it and unperturbed
By the moth that lies there littered,

And notice how the trees
Which took on anonymity
Are again in their huge histories
Displayed, that wherever we
Attempt, and as far as we can see,

The flowers everywhere
Are withering, the stars dissolved,
Amalgamated in a glare,
Which last night were revolved
Discreetly round us – and, involved,

The two of us, in these
Which early morning has deformed,
Must hope that in new properties
We'll find a uniform
To know each other truly by, or,

At the least, that these will,
When we rise, be seen with dawn
As remnant yet part raiment still,
Like flags that linger on
The sky when king and queen are gone.

NO CONTINUING CITY

My hands here, gentle, where her breasts begin,
My picture in her eyes –
It is time for me to recognise
This new dimension, my last girl.
So, to set my house in order, I imagine
Photographs, advertisements – the old lies,
The lumber of my soul –

All that is due for spring cleaning,
Everything that soul-destroys.
Into the open I bring
Girls who linger still in photostat
(For whom I was so many different boys) –
I explode their myths before it is too late,
Their promises I detonate –

There is quite a lot that I can do . . .
I leave them – are they six or seven, two or three? –
Locked in their small geographies.
The hillocks of their bodies' lovely shires
(Whose all weathers I have walked through)

Acre by acre recede entire
To summer country.

From collision to eclipse their case is closed.
Who took me by surprise
Like comets first – now, failing to ignite,
They constellate such uneventful skies,
Their stars arranged each night
In the old stories
Which I successfully have diagnosed.

Though they momentarily survive
In my delays,
They neither cancel nor improve
My continuing city with old ways,
Familiar avenues to love –
Down my one-way streets (it is time to finish)
Their eager syllables diminish.

Though they call out from the suburbs
Of experience – they know how that disturbs! –
Or, already tending towards home,
Prepare to hitch-hike on the kerbs,
Their bags full of dear untruths –
I am their medium
And I take the words out of their mouths.

From today new hoardings crowd my eyes,
Pasted over my ancient histories
Which (I must be cruel to be kind)
Only gale or cloudburst now discover,
Ripping the billboard of my mind –
Oh, there my lovers,
There my dead no longer advertise.

I transmit from the heart a closing broadcast
To my girl, my bride, my

wife-to-be –
I tell her she is welcome,
Advising her to make this last,
To be sure of finding room in me
(I embody bed and breakfast) –
To eat and drink me out of house and home.

LOVE POEM

I

You define with your perfume
Infinitely shifting zones
And print in falls of talcum
The shadow of your foot.

II

Gossamers spin from your teeth,
So many light constructions
Describing as with wet wings
The gully under my tongue.

III

These wide migrations begin
In our seamier districts –
A slumdweller's pigeons
Released from creaking baskets.

CARAVAN

A rickety chimney suggests
The diminutive stove,
Children perhaps, the pots
And pans adding up to love –

So much concentrated under
The low roof, the windows
Shuttered against snow and wind,
That you would be magnified

(If you were there) by the dark,
Wearing it like an apron
And revolving in your hands
As weather in a glass dome,

The blizzard, the day beyond
And – tiny, barely in focus –
Me disappearing out of view
On probably the only horse,

Cantering off to the right
To collect the week's groceries,
Or to be gone for good
Having drawn across my eyes

Like a curtain all that light
And the snow, my history
Stiffening with the tea towels
Hung outside the door to dry.

THE ROPE-MAKERS

Sometimes you and I are like rope-makers
Twisting straw into a golden cable,
So gradual my walking backwards
You fail to notice when I reach the door,
Each step infinitesimal, a delay,
Neither a coming nor a going when
Across the lane-way I face you still
Or, at large at last in the sunny fields,
Struggle to pick you out of the darkness

Where, close to the dresser, the scrubbed table,
Fingers securing the other end, you
Watch me diminish in a square of light.

SWANS MATING

Even now I wish that you had been there
Sitting beside me on the riverbank:
The cob and his pen sailing in rhythm
Until their small heads met and the final
Heraldic moment dissolved in ripples.

This was a marriage and a baptism,
A holding of breath, nearly a drowning,
Wings spread wide for balance where he trod,
Her feathers full of water and her neck
Under the water like a bar of light.

THE SWIM

The little rowing boat was full of
Friends and their intelligent children,
One of them bailing out for dear life
It seemed, while with an indolent hand

Another trailed a V on the lake
And directed it towards the island
Like an arrow. And nobody looked
As we undressed quickly and jumped in.

All of you vanished except your head:
Shoulders dissolving, and your arms too,
So opaque the element which could,
I knew, bend a stick at the elbow

Or, taking the legs from under you,
In its cat's-cradle of cross-currents
Like a bridegroom lift you bodily
Over the threshold to the island.

To risk brambles and nettles because
We wanted to make love there and then
In spite of the mud between my toes,
The weeds showing like veins on your skin,

Did seem all that remained to be done
As the creak of the rowlocks faded
And our friends left us to be alone
Or whatever they had decided.

LOVE POEM

If my nose could smell only
You and what you are about,
If my fingertips, tongue, mouth
Could trace your magnetic lines,
Your longitudes, latitudes,
If my eyes could see no more
Than dust accumulating
Under your hair, your skin's
Removals and departures,
The glacial progression
Of your fingernails, toenails,
If my ears could hear nothing
But the noise of your body's
Independent processes,
Lungs, heartbeat, intestines,
Then I would be lulled in sleep
That soothes for a lifetime
The scabby knees of boyhood,
And alters the slow descent
Of the scrotum towards death.

THE LINEN INDUSTRY

Pulling up flax after the blue flowers have fallen
And laying our handfuls in the peaty water
To rot those grasses to the bone, or building stooks
That recall the skirts of an invisible dancer,

We become a part of the linen industry
And follow its processes to the grubby town
Where fields are compacted into window-boxes
And there is little room among the big machines.

But even in our attic under the skylight
We make love on a bleach green, the whole meadow
Draped with material turning white in the sun
As though snow reluctant to melt were our attire.

What's passion but a battering of stubborn stalks,
Then a gentle combing out of fibres like hair
And a weaving of these into christening robes,
Into garments for a marriage or funeral?

Since it's like a bereavement once the labour's done
To find ourselves last workers in a dying trade,
Let flax be our matchmaker, our undertaker,
The provider of sheets for whatever the bed –

And be shy of your breasts in the presence of death,
Say that you look more beautiful in linen
Wearing white petticoats, the bow on your bodice
A butterfly attending the embroidered flowers.

PATCHWORK

I

There are ribbons that hold you together,
Hooks and eyes, hollows at the collarbone,

As though you dismantle your skeleton
Before stepping out of the crumpled ring,

Your nipples under my fingertips
Like white flowers on a white ground.

II

I pull up over us old clothes, remnants,
Stitching together shirts and nightshirts

Into such a dazzle as will burn away
Newspapers, letters, previous templates,

The hearth too, a red patch at the centre
That scorches the walls and our low ceiling.

AN AMISH RUG

As if a one-room schoolhouse were all we knew
And our clothes were black, our underclothes black,
Marriage a horse and buggy going to church
And the children silhouettes in a snowy field,

I bring you this patchwork like a smallholding
Where I served as the hired boy behind the harrow,
Its threads the colour of cantaloupe and cherry
Securing hay bales, corn cobs, tobacco leaves.

You may hang it on the wall, a cathedral window,
Or lay it out on the floor beside our bed
So that whenever we undress for sleep or love
We shall step over it as over a flowerbed.

SEAMUS DEANE
b. 1940

SOMETHING FAITHLESS

There's something faithless in my touch,
I glance disloyally and much
Has to be forgiven. Yet I clutch

The pillow when you stay away,
I never sleep; instead I play
Music until it's incongruous. I say

A million things into a phone
That's throbbing miles away.
I imagine you alone
On an ice-filled day
And I wish my touch
Had the fidelity of stone.

THE KISS

The bias of the sky,
Given away by the stars,
Is leaning from our window
Towards dawn.

Even my hand is coloured
By the whiskey glass
To that shade of feeling
We had a moment past.

Nothing is itself in love.
The very buildings in the water

In their shaky semitones
Have temperaments and alter.

This comic prejudice
Makes me feel that fact
Can never know endurance
Unless I counteract

Its bias and its frailties
With a love like this.
The ghosts of my perceptions
Take flesh upon a kiss.

MICHAEL HARTNETT

b. 1941

from ANATOMY OF A CLICHÉ

VII

I was sent away,
as always in this country.
pigeons rose with whistles
on their talons
and I heard you talk
a thousand times
in their sad whistlings.
'the snow is gone
the cherry trees
drop white petals
cold as snow
on my face.
O will I ever see you again?'

IX

her iron beats
the smell of bread
from damp linen,
silver, crystal
and warm white things:
whatever bird
I used to be,
hawk or lapwing,
tern, or something
wild, fierce or shy
these birds are dead
and I come here

on tiring wings.
odours of bread . . . .

I THINK SOMETIMES

I think sometimes
of the fingernail slotted
to most sensitive red flesh.
I think of it
ripped out, broken and made raw
with a bone-contracting pain.
Naked, bleeding,
white concave of hard dermis
and its red, moist groove of pain.
Death or going
away of you is all this,
the break of a fingernail
from a finger,
your mooncapped fingers lucid
to blood beneath, my own blood,
Oh my sweet wife!

DEREK MAHON
b. 1941

FORD MANOR
Non sapei tu che qui è l'uom felice?

Even on the quietest days the distant
Growl of cars remains persistent,
Reaching us in this airy box
We share with the field-mouse and the fox;
But she drifts in maternity blouses
Among crack-paned greenhouses –
A smiling Muse come back to life,
Part child, part mother, and part wife.

Even on the calmest nights the fitful
Prowl of planes is seldom still
Where Gatwick tilts to guide them home
From Tokyo, New York or Rome;
Yet even today the earth disposes
Bluebells, roses and primroses,
The dawn throat-whistle of a thrush
Deep in the dripping lilac bush.

THE OLD SNAPS

I keep your old snaps in my bottom drawer –
The icons of a more than personal love.
Look, three sisters out of Chekhov
('When will we ever go to Moscow?')
Ranged on the steps of the school-house
Where their mother is head teacher,
Out on the rocks, or holding down their hair
In a high wind on a North Antrim shore.

Later, yourself alone among sand-hills
Striking a slightly fictional pose,
Life-ready and impervious to harm
In your wind-blown school uniform
While the salt sea air fills
Your young body with ozone
And fine sand trickles into your shoes.
I think I must have known you even then.

We went to Moscow, and we will again.
Meanwhile we walk on the strand
And smile as if for the first time
While the children play in the sand.
We have never known a worse winter
But the old snaps are always there,
Framed for ever in your heart and mine
Where no hands can twist or tear.

from OVID IN LOVE

1

AMORES I, V

The day being humid and my head
heavy, I stretched out on a bed.
The open window to my right
reflected woodland-watery light,
a keyed-up silence as of dawn
or dusk, the vibrant and uncertain
hour when a brave girl might undress
and caper naked on the grass.
You entered in a muslin gown,
bare-footed, your fine braids undone,
a fabled goddess with an air
as if in heat yet debonair.
Aroused, I grabbed and roughly tore

until your gown squirmed on the floor.
Oh, you resisted, but like one
who knows resistance is in vain;
and, when you stood revealed, my eyes
feasted on shoulders, breasts and thighs.
I held you hard and down you slid
beside me, as we knew you would.
Oh, come to me again as then you did!

JOE SHEERIN
b. 1941

THE LOVER

Early in spring my father went courting
Death's daughter. He shaved a blush
Into his thin jaw, slyly went for walks
Alone at dusk. We observed them dimly
Behind hedges, heard them whisper in the barn.
His face was damp and his meat often lay
Untouched on his plate. We sensed romance.

Hurtful after his solid faithfulness; his stubbled
Kisses and his quiet words were sacraments
(love had his small-meshed net about our house then),
Not easily spat out or reneged on in the night.

Exhausted from watching we dozed inevitably
And he eloped into the blustery night with
No moon and the scutching wind on his thin
Nightdress. He woke up deceived. In a single

Bed in a dark church I saw him last lying. A candle
Winked and I recognised her passionless eye
And her hair wisping like roots around the pillows.

That night I kissed my children greedily, held
My wife close, promised love for ever. An old
Vow. Somehow, by God, I meant to keep it.

THE LEMAN

The letter I wrote you in invisible ink
Clarifies my love. It will betray its message

Having first been soaked in lemon – one
Stolen from a market stall should suffice –
And gently heated by your breath. Do not kiss
Or place it under your armpit. Keep some distance.
And remember it will not yield to milk or whey.

Fallen into the wrong hands an unmarked sheet
Means no love lost. Let them disbelieve.
Having read the message and understood, destroy
Like a good agent, the evidence. Ball tightly
In your fist and eat tearing word from word.
Swallow completely before continuing your walk.

Try not to wince remembering it's the bitterness
Of the lemon's nature that's at fault not my words.

EILÉAN NÍ CHUILLEANÁIN

b. 1942

LAY YOUR ARMS ASIDE

Gentlest of women, put your weapons by,
Unless you want to ruin all mankind;
Leave the assault or I must make reply,
Proclaiming that you are murderously inclined.
Put by your armour, lay your darts to rest,
Hide your soft hair and all its devious ways:
To see it lie in coils upon your breast
Poisons all hope and mercilessly slays.

Protest you never murdered in your life;
You lie: your hand's smooth touch, your well-shaped knee
Destroy as easily as axe or knife.
Your breasts like new spring flowers, your naked side
– I cry for aid to heaven – conceal from me;
Let shame for the destruction you have made
Hide your bright eyes, your shining teeth, away;
If all our sighs and trembling and dismay
Can touch your heart or satisfy your pride,
Gentlest of women, lay your arms aside.

AFTER THE IRISH of Pierce Ferriter, 17th century

AUGUSTUS YOUNG
b. 1943

from DÁNTA GRÁDHA

WOMAN, DON'T BE TROUBLESOME

Woman, don't be troublesome,
though your husband I may be;
our two minds were once at one,
why withdraw your hand from me?

Put your mouth of strawberry
on my mouth, cream is your cheek;
wind round white arms about me,
and do not go back to sleep.

Stay with me my flighty maid,
and be done with betrayal;
tonight this bed is well made,
let us toss it without fail.

Shut your eyes to other men,
no more women will I see:
the milkwhite tooth of passion
is between us – or should be.

AFTER THE IRISH (Anonymous, 15th–16th centuries)

EAVAN BOLAND

b. 1944

SONG

Where in blind files
Bats outsleep the frost
Water slips through stones
Too fast, too fast
For ice; afraid he'd slip
By me I asked him first.

Round as a bracelet
Clasping the wet grass,
An adder drowsed by berries
Which change blood to cess;
Dreading delay's venom
I risked the first kiss.

My skirt in my hand,
Lifting the hem high
I forded the river there;
Drops splashed my thigh.
Ahead of me at last
He turned at my cry:

'Look how the water comes
Boldly to my side;
See the waves attempt
What you have never tried.'
He late that night
Followed the leaping tide.

THE BOTANIC GARDENS

for Kevin

Guided by love, leaving aside dispute –
Guns on the pages of newspapers, the sound
Urgent of peace – we drive in real pursuit
Of another season, spring, where each has found
Something before, new, and then sense
In the Botanic Gardens, terms of reference.

You take my hand. Three years ago, your bride,
I felt your heart in darkness, a full moon
Hauling mine to it like a tide.
Still at night our selves reach to join.
To twine like these trees in peace and stress
Before the peril of unconsciousness.

Corsican pine, guerilla poison plants,
The first gardener here by foreign carriage
And careful seeding in this circumference
Imitated the hours of our marriage:
The flowers of forced proximity, swollen, fed,
Flourishing here, usually sheltered,

Exposed this once. Now you have overstepped
My reach, searching for something this February
Like a scholar in poor light over a script,
Able at last to decipher its coded story
And so preoccupied you do not see
My absence in the conservatory

Where you, while African grotesqueries
Sweat in sandy heat, at last stand
Wondering at cacti, deformed trees
Most ridicule. Each pumpkin history
Turns coach at a touch of your hand.
I watch and love you in your mystery.

PAUL DURCAN

b. 1944

NESSA

I met her on the First of August
In the Shangri-La Hotel,
She took me by the index finger
And dropped me in her well.
And that was a whirlpool, that was a whirlpool,
And I very nearly drowned.

Take off your pants, she said to me,
And I very nearly didn't;
Would you care to swim, she said to me,
And I hopped into the Irish sea.
And that was a whirlpool, that was a whirlpool,
And I very nearly drowned.

On the way back I fell in the field
And she fell down beside me.
I'd have lain in the grass with her all my life
With Nessa:
She was a whirlpool, she was a whirlpool,
And I very nearly drowned.

Oh Nessa my dear, Nessa my dear,
Will you stay with me on the rocks?
Will you come for me into the Irish sea
And for me let your red hair down?
And then we will ride into Dublin city
In a taxi-cab wrapped-up in dust.
Oh you are a whirlpool, you are a whirlpool,
And I am very nearly drowned.

MAKING LOVE OUTSIDE ÁRAS AN UACHTARÁIN

When I was a boy, myself and my girl
Used bicycle up to the Phoenix Park;
Outside the gates we used lie in the grass
Making love outside Áras an Uachtaráin.

Often I wondered what de Valera would have thought
Inside in his ivory tower
If he knew that we were in his green, green grass
Making love outside Áras an Uachtaráin.

Because the odd thing was – oh how odd it was –
We both revered Irish patriots
And we dreamed our dreams of a green, green flag
Making love outside Áras an Uachtaráin.

But even had our names been Diarmaid and Gráinne
We doubted de Valera's approval
For a poet's son and a judge's daughter
Making love outside Áras an Uachtaráin.

I see him now in the heat-haze of the day
Blindly stalking us down;
And, levelling an ancient rifle, he says 'Stop
Making love outside Áras an Uachtaráin.'

THE JEWISH BRIDE

after Rembrandt

At the black canvas of estrangement,
As the smoke empties from the ruins under a gold
  Winter sky,
Death-trains clattering across the back gardens of
  Amsterdam

– Sheds, buckets, wire, concrete
– Manholes, pumps, pliers, scaffolding;
I see, as if for the first time,
The person you were, and are, and always will be
Despite the evil that men do:
The teenage girl on the brink of womanhood
Who, when I met you, was on the brink of everything –
Composing fairytales and making drawings
That used remind your friends of Anderson and Thurber –
Living your hidden life that promised everything
Despite all the maimed, unreliable men and women
Who were at that moment congregating all around you:
Including, of course, most of all, myself.
You made of your bedroom a flowing stream
Into which, daily, you threw proofs of your dreams;
Pinned to your bedroom wall with brass-studded
  drawing pins
Newspaper and magazine photographs of your heroes and
  heroines.
People who met you breathed the air of freedom,
And sensuality fragile as it was wild:
'Nessa's air makes free' people used say,
Like in the dark ages, 'Town air makes free'.
The miracle is that you survived me.
You stroll about the malls and alleyways of Amsterdam,
About its islands and bridges, its archways and jetties,
With Spring in your heels, although it is Winter;
Privately, publicly, along the Grand Parade;
A Jewish Bride who has survived the death-camp,
Free at last of my swastika eyes
Staring at you from across spiked dinner plates
Or from out of the bunker of a TV armchair;
Free of the glare off my jackboot silence;
Free of the hysteria of my gestapo voice;
Now your shyness replenished with all your old cheeky
  confidence –
That grassy well at which red horses used rear up and sip

With young men naked riding bareback calling your name.
Dog-muzzle of tension torn down from your face;
Black polythene of asphyxiation peeled away from your
soul;
Your green eyes quivering with dark, sunny laughter
And – all spread-eagled and supple again – your loving,
freckled hands.

AROUND THE CORNER FROM FRANCIS BACON

Around the corner from Francis Bacon
Was where we made our first nest together
On the waters of the flood;
Where we first lived in sin:
The sunniest, most virtuous days of our life.
Not even the pastoral squalor of Clapham Common
Nor the ghetto life of Notting Hill Gate
Nor the racial drama of Barcelona
Nor the cliffhanging bourgeois life of Cork City
Could ever equal those initial, primeval times together
Living in sin
In the halcyon ambience of South Kensington,
A haven for peaceful revolutionaries such as Harriet Waugh
Or Francis Bacon, or ourselves.
I slept on an ironing board in the kitchen
And you slept in the attic:
Late at night when all the other flat-dwellers
Were abed and – we thought wishfully – asleep,
You crept down the attic ladder
To make love with me on the ironing board,
As if we had known each other in a previous life
So waterily did our two body-phones attune,
Underwater swimming face to face in the dark,
Francis Bacon-Cimabue style.
My body-phone was made in Dublin
But your body-phone was made in Japan.

Standing up naked on the kitchen floor,
In the smog-filtered moonlight,
You placed your hand on my little folly, murmuring:
I have come to iron you, Sir Board.
Far from the tyrant liberties of Dublin, Ireland,
Where the comedy of freedom was by law forbidden
And truth, since the freedom of the state, gone
  underground.
When you had finished ironing me
I felt like hot silk queueing up to be bathèd
Under a waterfall in Samarkand
Or a mountain stream in Enniskerry.
Every evening I waited for you to come home,
Nipping out only in the rush hour to the delicatessen
Where Francis Bacon, basket under arm,
Surfacing like Mr Mole from his mews around the corner,
Used be stocking up in tomato purée and curry powder
Before heading off into the night and 'The Colony Room
  Club'
Into whose green dark you and I sometimes also tip-toed.
In your own way you were equally Beatrix Potter-like,
Coming home to me laden with fish fingers and baked
  beans.
While I read to you from Dahlberg, you taught me about the
  psyche
Of the female orang-outang caged in the zoo:
Coronation Street . . . *Z Cars* . . . *The World in Action* . . .
Then Z Cars to beat all Z Cars – our own world in action –
The baskets of your eyes chock-a-block with your unique
  brands
Of tomato purée and curry powder;
Or, *That Was The Week That Was*, and then, my sleeping
  friend,
In the sandhills of whose shoulders sloping secretly down
Into small, hot havens of pure unscathèd sands
Where the only sounds are the sounds of the sea's tidal
  waters

Flooding backwards and forwards,
Tonight is the night that always is forever –
Ten or twenty minutes in the dark,
And in four million years or so
My stomach will swarm again suddenly with butterflies,
As with your bowl of water and your towel,
Your candle and your attic ladder,
Your taut high wire and your balancing pole,
A green mini-dress over your arm, a Penguin paperback in
your hand,
I watch you coming towards me in the twilight of rush hour
On your hands and knees
And on the wet, mauve tip of your extended tongue
The two multi-coloured birds of your plumed eyes ablaze
Around the corner from Francis Bacon.

RAYMOND OF THE ROOFTOPS

The morning after the night
The roof flew off the house
And our sleeping children narrowly missed
Being decapitated by falling slates,
I asked my husband if he would
Help me put back the roof:
But no – he was too busy at his work
Writing for a women's magazine in London
An Irish Fairytale called *Raymond of the Rooftops*.
Will you have a heart, woman – he bellowed –
Can't you see I am up to my eyes and ears in work,
Breaking my neck to finish *Raymond of the Rooftops*,
Fighting against time to finish *Raymond of the Rooftops*,
Putting everything I have got into *Raymond of the Rooftops?*

Isn't it well for him? *Everything he has got!*

All I wanted him to do was to stand
For an hour, maybe two hours, three at the most,
At the bottom of the stepladder
And hand me up slates while I slated the roof:
But no – once again I was proving to be the insensitive,
Thoughtless, feckless even, wife of the artist.
There was I up to my fat, raw knees in rainwater
Worrying him about the hole in our roof
While he was up to his neck in *Raymond of the Rooftops*.
Will you have a heart, woman – he bellowed –
Can't you see I am up to my eyes and ears in work,
Breaking my neck to finish *Raymond of the Rooftops*,
Fighting against time to finish *Raymond of the Rooftops*,
Putting everything I have got into *Raymond of the Rooftops?*

Isn't it well for him? *Everything he has got!*

THE PIETÀ'S OVER

The Pietà's Over – and, now, my dear, droll, husband,
As middle age tolls its bell along the via dolorosa of life,
It is time for you to get down off my knees
And learn to walk on your own two feet.
I will admit it is difficult for a man of forty
Who has spent all his life reclining in his wife's lap,
Being given birth to by her again and again, year in, year
out,
To stand on his own two feet, but it has to be done –
Even if at the end of the day he commits harikari.
A man cannot be a messiah for ever,
Messiahing about in his wife's lap,
Suffering fluently in her arms,
Flowing up and down in the lee of her bosom,
Forever being mourned for by the eternal feminine,
Being keened over every night of the week for sixty mortal
years.

The Pietà's Over – it is Easter over all our lives:
The revelation of our broken marriage, and its resurrection;
The breaking open of the tomb, and the setting free.
Painful as it was for me, I put you down off my knee
And I showed you the door.
Although you pleaded with me to keep you on my knee
And to mollycoddle you, humour you, within the family
 circle
('Don't put me out into the cold world' you cried),
I did not take the easy way out and yield to you –
Instead I took down the door off its hinges
So that the sunlight shone all the more squarely
Upon the pure, original brokenness of our marriage;
I whispered to you, quietly, yet audibly,
For all the diaspora of your soul to hear:
The Pietà's Over.

Yet even now, one year later, you keep looking back
From one side of Europe to the other,
Gaping at my knees as if my knees
Were the source of all that you have been, are, or will be.
By all means look around you, but stop looking back.
I would not give you shelter if you were homeless in the
 streets
For you must make your home in yourself, and not in a
 woman.
Keep going out the road for it is only out there –
Out there where the river achieves its riverlessness –
That you and I can become at last strangers to one another,
Ready to join up again on Resurrection Day.
Therefore, I must keep whispering to you, over and over:
My dear loved one, I have to tell you
You have run the gamut of piety –
The Pietà's Over.

THE TURKISH CARPET

No man could have been more unfaithful
To his wife than me;
Scarcely a day passed
That I was not unfaithful to her.
I would be in the living-room ostensibly reading or writing
When she'd come home from work unexpectedly early
And, popping her head round the door, find me
  wrapped round
A figure of despair.
It would not have been too bad if I'd been wrapped round
Another woman –that would have been infidelity of a kind
With which my wife could have coped.
What she could not cope with, try as she did,
Was the infidelity of unhope,
The personal betrayal of universal despair.
When my wife called to me from the living-room door
Tremblingly ajar, with her head peering round it,
– The paintwork studded with headwounds and
  knuckleprints –
Called to me across the red, red grass of home
– *The Turkish Carpet* –
Which her gay mother had given us as a wedding present
(And on which our children had so often played
Dolls' Houses on their hands and knees
And headstands and cartwheels and dances,
And on which we ourselves had so often made love),
I clutched my despair to my breast
And with brutality kissed it – Sweet Despair –
Staring red-eyed down at *The Turkish Carpet* .
O my dear husband, will you not be faithful to me?
Have I not given you hope all the days of my life?

THE BERLIN WALL CAFÉ

Once we were Berlin – you and I . . .
Until an agèd priest,
As shepherdlike a pastor as one could hope to meet
In the neon forest –
Father Boniface –
Married us with a gun.
Tears of joy were in his eyes as, with a flick of his wrist
(All mottled and bluey)
He waved his pistol in the air, firing gaily:
A long white wall unfurled from it,
Trailing its roll-top and its graffiti.

Thus it was we pitched our tent in the continuing city:
Ecstatically lonely together in a two-room flat
In Bernauer Strasse beside the Berlin Wall,
Around the corner from the open-air table tennis tables
In Swinemünder Strasse,
Handy for the *U-Bahn* in Volta Strasse.
I counted myself the luckiest man alive in Berlin
To be marooned with you:
You – incarnate coincidence of the beautiful and the true –
All risk and give –
Reticent woman whose eyes were caves
Concealed in cascades of red hair.
Yet all I could talk about was the Berlin Wall
As if the Berlin Wall was more important than you!
On the night you gave birth to our child
I was too busy to attend – addressing a meeting
On the Berlin Wall!
When I should have been cooking your supper
After your long day's work in the office in Spandau,
I was manning the Observation Platforms –
Making faces at the *Volkspolizei!*

At the end of 1980,
When I should have been minding our marriage
And concentrating on loving you,
All I could consider was whether or not
I should become Editor of the *Berlin Wall Gazette:*
I was a most proper Charlie!
No wonder that your friends could not abide me!
Whenever they saw me approaching they scattered:
'Watch out – here he comes – Checkpoint Charlie.'

In 1984 you could stand it no more:
You escaped from West Berlin
Into East Berlin – where you are free of me
And of the Show Biz of the Free Democracies
Advertising Unemployment and All That Jazz.
Purple with envy, I hear you have teamed up
With an all-woman jazz combo in Unter den Linden.
They say there's no more exciting woman in Berlin
Than when you're alone on the high-hat cymbals
To beat the band in the Berlin Wall Café:
Once we were Berlin – you and I . . .

AT THE FUNERAL OF THE MARRIAGE

At the funeral of the marriage
My wife and I paced
On either side of the hearse,
Our children racing behind it . . .
As the coffin was emptied
Down into the bottomless grave,
Our children stood in a half-circle,
Playing on flutes and recorders.
My wife and I held hands.
While the mourners wept and the gravediggers
Unfurled shovelfuls of clay
Down on top of the coffin,

We slowly walked away,
Accomplices beneath the yew trees.
We had a cup of tea in the graveyard café
Across the street from the gates:
We discussed the texture of the undertaker's face,
Its beetroot quality.
As I gazed at my wife
I wondered who on earth she was –
I saw that she was a green-eyed stranger.
I said to her: Would you like to go to a film?
She said: I would love to go to a film.
In the back seats of the cinema,
As we slid up and down in our seats
In a frenzy of hooks and clasps,
The manager courteously asked us not to take off our clothes.
We walked off urgently through the rain-strewn streets
Into a leaf-sodden cul-de-sac
And as, from the tropic isle of our bed,
Chock-a-block with sighs & cries,
We threw our funeral garments on the floor,
We could hear laughter outside the door.
There is no noise children love more to hear
Than the noise of their parents making love:
O my darling, who on earth are you?

MICHAEL FOLEY
b. 1947

from TRUE LIFE LOVE STORIES

16

Sois sage, ô ma doleur . . . I don't
hate the young anymore.
Let them greet with satirical
signs of the cross

and smirk of their 'impecunious state'.
I won't hate them
anymore. Love's the boyo to
see them all straight,

so I muse, for I'm soft as an
inside leg this year,
all due to woman's passive power.
Entends, ma chère,

this song and soft clip-clop is me.
It's you I trot to,
tired and tame, melodious with
new-found gallantry.

THE IN-BETWEEN SONG

It's falling in love people love, the nervous excitement
Move and counter-move in the ancient game of enticement

But I don't yearn for early days with their permanent state
Of tumescence, prepared to get up on a cracked plate

Smoothtalking my way into your house and fumbling on chairs
Jumping away in fright at a bronchial cough upstairs

Returning through dark deserted streets, pounding on like crack
Troops on the march – or hobbling in agony, foreskin back

Getting home again at dawn and trying not to wake a soul
By peeing in total darkness down the side of the bowl.

Nor do I yearn to be free, casting off wasted years
To ride someone else into the sunset with joyful tears.

So that's NO bap-faced students, NO culture vultures in heat
NO colleagues or in-laws seeing my true worth, *NO dark meat*

NO petulant nymphets, detached and impossibly slim
NO mature divorcees with it biting the leg off them

NO receptionists taking off glasses and letting down hair
NO frustrated green-belt wives in expensive underwear

– Strictly for Wednesday Plays. Real ones are tough as old hide.
There's little glamour truly. As my old friend gently sighed

Of Marilyn Monroe: *How could the Kennedy boys get*
Excited? Her poor little thing wouldn't even be wet.

Then there's phoney free-form passion, ripping skin and yelling.
I favour standards, traditional grammar and spelling

Calm organisation and planning, the disciplined way
(See my 'Top-down Methodology in Structured Sex Play').

You're my centre of excellence with private grounds in bloom
Resource and reception areas, hospitality room

My new in-house system with hands-on capability
User-friendly, with feedback, power and flexibility

Affording continuous two-way communication
My optimal target group for market penetration

My core- and flexi-time, my rest and recreation
My ongoing, upwardly mobile situation.

My love will survive all troubles, the fighting and bitching
Huffs, depressions, illnesses and personal-membrane itching

The ravages of time, of course. Decrepit, fat or thin
I will never be unsure which wrinkle to put it in.

Tumultuous, piquant, the start and the end of the thing
Are the bits that sell – but the in-between time's what I sing

The lights low and half the band gone for their tea and a bun.
We take the floor again. The number is a smoochy one.

TOM PAULIN

b. 1949

PERSONAL COLUMN

These messages are secret, the initials
Code them, puzzling most of us. 'LY
Where are you now? I love you still. MN'.
And then, next evening, 'MN are you still there?
Loving you. LY.' Until, 'Shall I write
To old address?' MN suggests, waiting.

Each teatime, the thin signals start again.
You can almost hear the cheeping
Of separated loves, obscure adulteries
That finished in pub carparks, though they want
To make it new, to meet again, furtively,
Like spies whose thoughts touch before their bodies can.

Love, in an empty warehouse, might be like this.
To think small print, so public, can be tender.
Who'd guess that in a city where the news
Is normal, so many men and women wait
For the paper-boy, their go-between, to bring them
Lonely but hopeful, to a bed somewhere?

A LYRIC AFTERWARDS

There was a taut dryness all that summer
and you sat each day in the hot garden
until those uniformed comedians
filled the street with their big white ambulance,
fetching you and bringing you back to me.

Far from the sea of ourselves we waited
and prayed for the tight blue silence to give.
In your absence I climbed to a square room
where there were dried flowers, folders of sonnets
and crossword puzzles: call them musical

snuffboxes or mannered anachronisms,
they were all too uselessly intricate,
caskets of the dead spirit. Their bitter
constraints and formal pleasures were a style
of being perfect in despair; they spoke

with the vicious trapped crying of a wren.
But that is changed now, and when I see you
walking by the river, a step from me,
there is this great kindness everywhere:
now in the grace of the world and always.

MEDBH McGUCKIAN
b. 1950

THE HOLLYWOOD BED

We narrow into the house, the room, the bed,
Where sleep begins its shunting. You adopt
Your mask, your intellectual cradling of the head,
Neat as notepaper in your creaseless
Envelope of clothes, while I lie crosswise,
Imperial as a favoured only child,
Calmed by sagas of how we lay like spoons
In a drawer, till you blew open
My tightened bud, my fully-buttoned housecoat,
Like some Columbus mastering
The saw-toothed waves, the rows of letter 'm's.

Now the headboard is disturbed
By your uncomfortable skew, your hands
Like stubborn adverbs visiting your face,
Or your shoulder, in your piquancy of dreams,
The outline that if you were gone,
Would find me in your place.

THE APHRODISIAC

She gave it out as if it were
A marriage or a birth, some other
Interesting family event, that she
Had finished sleeping with him, that
Her lover was her friend. It was his heart
She wanted, the bright key to his study,
Not the menacings of love. So he is
Banished to his estates, to live
Like a man in a glasshouse; she has taken to

A little cap of fine white lace
In the mornings, feeds her baby
In a garden you could visit blindfold
For its scent alone:
                    But though a ray of grace
Has fallen, all her books seem as frumpish
As the last year's gambling game, when she
Would dress in pink taffeta, and drive
A blue phaeton, or in blue, and drive
A pink one, with her black hair supported
By a diamond comb, floating about
Without panniers. How his most
Caressing look, his husky whisper suffocates her,
This almost perfect power of knowing
More than a kept woman. The between-maid
Tells me this is not the only secret staircase.
Rumour has it she's taken to rouge again.

TO THE NIGHTINGALE

I remember our first night in this grey
And paunchy house: you were still slightly
In love with me, and dreamt of having
A grown son, your body in the semi-gloom
Turning my dead layers into something
Resembling a rhyme. That smart and
Cheerful rain almost beat the hearing
Out of me, and yet I heard my name
Pronounced in a whisper as a June day
Will force itself into every room.

To the nightingale it made no difference
Of course, that you tossed about an hour,
Two hours, till what was left of your future
Began: nor to the moon that nearly rotted,
Like the twenty-first century growing

Its grass through me. But became in the end,
While you were still asleep, a morning
Where I saw our neighbours' mirabelle,
Bent over our hedge, and its trespassing
Fruit, unacknowledged as our own.

THE SITTING

My half-sister comes to me to be painted:
She is posing furtively, like a letter being
Pushed under a door, making a tunnel with her
Hands over her dull-rose dress. Yet her coppery
Head is as bright as a net of lemons, I am
Painting it hair by hair as if she had not
Disowned it, or forsaken those unsparkling
Eyes as blue may be sifted from the surface
Of a cloud; and she questions my brisk
Brushwork, the note of positive red
In the kissed mouth I have given her,
As a woman's touch makes curtains blossom
Permanently in a house: she calls it
Wishfulness, the failure of the tampering rain
To go right into the mountain, she prefers
My sea-studies, and will not sit for me
Again, something half-opened, rarer
Than railroads, a soiled red-letter day.

ON NOT BEING YOUR LOVER

Your eyes were ever brown, the colour
Of time's submissiveness. Love nerves
Or a heart, beat in their world of
Privilege, I had not yet kissed you
On the mouth.

But I would not say, in my un-freedom
I had weakly drifted there, like the
Bone-deep blue that visits and decants
The eyes of our children:

How warm and well-spaced their dreams
You can tell from the sleep-late mornings
Taken out of my face! Each lighted
Window shows me cardiganed, more desolate
Than the garden, and more hallowed
Than the hinge of the brass-studded
Doors that we close, and no one opens,
That we open and no one closes.

In a far-flung, too young part,
I remembered all your slender but
Persistent volume said, friendly, complex
As the needs of your new and childfree girl.

PARTLY DEDICATED TO A HOUSE

Afraid of the window's glance all blue
And despairing, I press home the crisis
It imposes; and the taste I'd like you
To have found there turns our love
Into the same thirsty act of contemplation.

Not so long ago, words spoken too soon,
Such as 'It really is over', prolonged
Themselves in prearranged silences
Like inert stations on a line. And
Though it was in essence anything but over,
These are the places I now prefer, the
Farmyard where we had fallen out
Swept clean and hungrier.

Leave your letter for five hours on a
Blotting-pad to isolate and then add
Which one of us is writing to which,
Expecting an imaginary reply.

PETER FALLON

b. 1951

CAROLINA

You fiddle with the TV set.
You check the view.
They're all the same, these rooms,
all almost new.

They're rented cars. They do.
They've carried you to ecstasy, beds of blame.
You've told her things you thought you'd tell
no one. You've called her by another's name.

And she who was so innocent
has brought a change of clothes.
DO NOT DISTURB and still the porter knocks
with coffee. You *know* he knows.

And was so shy now showers with the door
ajar. You marvel at her wet panache.
You'll leave no proper names or numbers.
You'll pay by cash.

She stands between the made and unmade bed
and starts to pack. *O tell*
no one she starts to say as she begins
to turn her back on this or that motel.

PAUL MULDOON

b. 1951

WIND AND TREE

In the way that the most of the wind
Happens where there are trees,

Most of the world is centred
About ourselves.

Often where the wind has gathered
The trees together and together,

One tree will take
Another in her arms and hold.

Their branches that are grinding
Madly together and together,

It is no real fire.
They are breaking each other.

Often I think I should be like
The single tree, going nowhere,

Since my own arm could not and would not
Break the other. Yet by my broken bones

I tell new weather.

WHIM

She was sitting with a pint and a small one
That afternoon in the Europa Hotel,

Poring over one of those old legends –
Cu Chulainn and the Birds of Appetite –
When he happened along, and took a pew.

'Pardon me, for I couldn't help but notice
You've got the O'Grady translation.'
'What of it? What's it to you?'
'Standish O'Grady? Very old-fashioned.
Cu Chulainn and the Birds of Appetite?
More like *How Cu Chulainn Got His End*.'
He smiled. She was smiling too.
'If you want the flavour of the original
You should be looking to Kuno Meyer.
As it happens, I've got the very edition
That includes this particular tale.
You could have it on loan, if you like,
If you'd like to call back to my place, now.'

Not that they made it as far as his place.
They would saunter through the Botanic Gardens
Where they held hands, and kissed,
And by and by one thing led to another.
To cut not a very long story short,
Once he got stuck into her he got stuck
Full stop.
They lay there quietly until dusk
When an attendant found them out.
He called an ambulance, and gently but firmly
They were manhandled on to a stretcher
Like the last of an endangered species.

QUOOF

How often have I carried our family word
for the hot water bottle
to a strange bed,

as my father would juggle a red-hot half-brick
in an old sock
to his childhood settle.
I have taken it into so many lovely heads
or laid it between us like a sword.

An hotel room in New York City
with a girl who spoke hardly any English,
my hand on her breast
like the smouldering one-off spoor of the yeti
or some other shy beast
that has yet to enter the language.

KISSING AND TELLING

Or she would turn up *The Songs of Leonard Cohen*
on the rickety old gramophone.

And you knew by the way she unbound her tresses
and stepped from her William Morris dresses

you might just as well be anyone.

Goat's-milk cheeses, Navajo rugs,
her reading aloud from *A Dictionary of Drugs* –

she made wine of almost everything.

How many of those she found out on the street
and fetched back to her attic room –

to promise nothing, to take nothing for granted –

how many would hold by the axiom
she would intone as though it were her mantra?

I could name names. I could be indiscreet.

AISLING

I was making my way home late one night
this summer, when I staggered
into a snow drift.

Her eyes spoke of a sloe-year,
her mouth a year of haws.

Was she Aurora, or the goddess Flora,
Artemidora, or Venus bright,
or Anorexia, who left
a lemon stain on my flannel sheet?

It's all much of a muchness.

In Belfast's Royal Victoria Hospital
a kidney machine
supports the latest hunger-striker
to have called off his fast, a saline
drip into his bag of brine.

A lick and a promise. Cuckoo spittle.
I hand my sample to Doctor Maw.
She gives me back a confident *All Clear.*

NUALA NÍ DHÓMHNAILL

b. 1952

I CANNOT LIE HERE

translation by Michael Hartnett

I cannot lie here anymore
in your aroma –
with your pillowed mouth
asnore,
your idle hand
across my hip
not really caring
whether I exist.

I'm not upset
because you ignore me
nor because our happy summer
washes over me –
it's not the bedside flowers
that intoxicate
but your body your aroma,
a blend of blood and earth.

I'll get up from the bed
and put on my clothes
and leave with the carkeys
from your fist stolen
and drive to the city.

At nine tomorrow
you'll get a call
telling you where to go
to pick up your car –
but I cannot lie here anymore

where your aroma laps –
because I'll fall in love with you,
(perhaps).

KISS

translation by Michael Hartnett

Straight on my mouth
another man's kiss.
He put his tongue
between my lips.
I was numb
and said to him
'Little man, go home
you're drunk
your wife waits at the door.'

But when I recall
your kiss
I shake, and all
that lies
between my hips
liquifies
to milk.

MASCULUS GIGANTICUS HIBERNICUS

translation by Michael Hartnett

Country lout, knife thrower (dagger-wielder)
whether in jeans or a devil at noon
all dolled up in your pinstriped suit
you're always after the one thing.

Dangerous relic from the Iron Age
you sit in pubs and devise
the treacherous plan
that does not recoil on you –
a vengeful incursion to female land.

Because you will not dare to halt the growth
of the dark red damask rose in your mother's heart
you will have to turn the garden
to a trampled mess
pounded and ruined by your two broad hooves.

And you're frisky, prancing, antlered –
your bread is baked.
You'd live off the furze
or the heather that grows
on a young girl's sunny slopes.

MEDB SPEAKS

translation by Michael Hartnett

War I declare from now
on all the men of Ireland
on all the corner-boys
lying curled in children's cradles
their willies worthless
wanting no woman
all macho boasting
last night they bedded
a Grecian princess –
a terrible war I will declare.

Merciless war I declare –
endless, without quarter
on the twenty-pint heroes
who sit on seats beside me

who nicely up my skirts put hands
no apology or reason
just looking for a chance
to dominate my limbs –
a merciless war I will declare!

I will make incursions
through the fertile land of Ireland
my battalions all in arms
my Amazons beside me
(not just to steal a bull
not over beasts this battle –
but for an honour-price
a thousand times more precious –
my dignity).
I will make fierce incursions.

THE SHANNON ESTUARY WELCOMING THE FISH

translation by Michael Hartnett

The leap of the salmon
in darkness,
naked blade
shield of silver.
I am welcoming, full of nets,
inveigling,
slippery with seaweed,
quiet eddies
and eel-tails.

This fish
is nothing but meat
with very few bones
and very few entrails;

twenty pounds of muscle tauted,
aimed
at its nest in the mossy place.

And I will sing a lullaby
to my love
wave upon wave
stave upon half-stave,
my phosphorescence as bed-linen under him,
my favourite, whom I, from afar have chosen.

WILLIAM PESKETT

b. 1952

WHY I AM THE LAST OF THE WORLD'S GREAT LOVERS

When shadowboxing in the Saturday backstalls
an extra feature sometimes flicks
across my mind.
It's a shame nobody seems to be wearing
clown lipstick anymore
or rolling soft make-eyes in silent scenes.
And nobody ever holds a girl
the way they used to.

Nobody does a silken swoon
across the railroad track anymore
or commits one of those flash
honkytonk suicides.

Everybody's forgotten that Valentino was once
the coming-soon at their local Odeon
and that his coffin was buried
in pink reincarnations and cards saying, come back, Valentino,
see you in heaven.

One day I'll request his second showing
with dubbed stereophonic keyboards
and fill the kinema with my children
announcing,
by way of explanation, that this
perhaps is why I
am the last of the world's great lovers.

UNDERWEAR

When the box arrived he was so proud
he told her to put them on straight away.
There was a row and talk about love
but in the end she conceded
the touch of the satin and the nylon lace,
the result of promised silk.
Fighting back the tears
she moved her limbs in the fantastic costume,
in a conventional way.

When all was quiet and his pride was gone
she left him on the bed
and carefully folded up the things.
Love, she thought, has elevated our view,
denying appetites that don't fit in the picture.
We've just moved in from the jungle,
covering our tracks.
Stopping in the bathroom to run the water
she stole a glance at the lover,
her cheeks wet with tears,
her red nipples spittle-wet.

WINDOW DRESSING

The beautiful man and his wife
must have fled,
deserting their immaculate husks
like wholesome insects
on a jagged flight to a new life.

The copies that remain possess everything.
In their still and vigilant life
of display they need cocktail cabinets

and sofas
but have no inclination to move over,

to touch and merge.
The actual people, lush and naked,
are hovering on transient wings:
they're making love
out of hours.

On dark nights, through the window
on their brilliant home
I see them returning,
sheepish and ashamed,
slipping back into shape.

THOMAS McCARTHY
b. 1954

IN THE LUXEMBOURG GARDENS

Nothing could be second-hand that's so full of love.
Although avenues are wrecked with tourists
In canvas shoes, afternoons full of Coke,
The dappled light of the chestnut grove
Is new, and the ludic patterns of the fountain.
The fresh dog mess on the gravel path is true
And full of words like *love, companionship, good news*.

In America, once, I heard the cicada in the trees,
A strange, continental, clicking sound, that made me feel
A total stranger. Until I recalled
The cicadas in the fields of Whitman, the cicadas
Among the empty oil-drums of Roethke. Such familial
Calls from the extensive parish of poems.

Walking with you in the Luxembourg Gardens, I heard
The childhood of many books whooping with joy;
I heard mothers giving a first-hand account of care.
I wondered which child was taking notes
For the first perfect biography of love –
We would be the passers-by in that first memory;
The Luxembourg in our talk, the chestnut light above.

THE DARK

You've spent the last few days
apart from me, chemically apart,
wandering from tray to tray.
Your hair has been tied back
like a Victorian woman's

bending under a reading lamp.
When I get a glimpse I see
your whole face screwed up
as if your eyes had come upon
a serious fictional event.

Can we talk? Can we talk?
Not now you whisper –
you are a nurse giving me
the correct visiting hours;
your chemical patients are
at their critical temperature.
The safety-light
is all you can go by
to see new portraits forming
in the agitated tray.

TOAST

No lovelier city than all of this,
Cork city, your early morning kiss;
peeled oranges and white porcelain,
midsummer Sunday mists
that scatter before breakfast.

Mass bells are pealing in every district,
in the Latin quarter of St Luke's,
the butter *quartier* of Blackpool.
Every brass appeal calls to prayer
our scattered books and utensils,

the newly blessed who've put on clothes.
Why have I been as lucky as this?
To have found one so meticulous
in love, so diffident yet close
that the house is charged with kinetic peace.

Like a secret lover, I should bring
you bowls of fresh roses, knowing
that you would show them how to thrive.
Lucky it's Sunday, or I'd have
to raid the meter for spare shillings!

Or, maybe I should wash my filthy socks,
fret at the curtain, iron clothes,
like you after Sunday breakfast.
Normal things run deep, God knows,
like love in flat-land, eggs on toast.

JULIE O'CALLAGHAN
b. 1954

OPALS

Lying on my stomach,
silk pillows underneath me,
I trace the outline
of each plum blossom
on my sleeve
and try to hide my face
from the other ladies
with the screen of my hair.
They are discussing the Prince,
gossiping about which royal robe
suits him best.
I have traced the flower six times now,
hoping they won't ask me my opinion
or notice the handful of opal teardrops
decorating my sleeve.

JANET SHEPPERSON

b. 1954

THE FIRST TIME

Woman A track set about with blossom brought us
over stones, perforating my tiredness,
to where the cottage brooded grey
under a hovering alien mountain
and I could not warm it with laughter.
Afraid of those rainswept spaces
I looked for comfort in your arms,
but you were too soon asleep,
remote, satisfied, you left me
to the sickly dawn, crows scraping the roof.
You expected lightness, and I
was clenched like a stone at your table.
I wouldn't climb the mountain with you –
miles of windy grass, your silences.

Man You were like a fern frond, curled up tight,
I thought you would feather out in a blazing of green
but you clung to me, brown and tired and reproachful.
I didn't know how to fill your emptiness, or why
you rejected my secret country, you wouldn't come
to see the ravens wheeling above the mountain,
the foxgloves under the rock, the waterfall,
grass with the wind singing through it, freedom.

Woman I wanted you to re-make
the nest of words and glances
you promised to lay me in.

Man You were like sad mud-flats
when the tide's gone out;
my feet sank in uncertainty.

Woman We sat by the sulky fire, unpicking
our net of defences, learning
that white ashes keep their warmth,
that silence is a tunnel
of rushing air and heartbeats,
that smoke has its own rhythm
and the catch in your voice is a spark
for the flame in mine.

SEÁN DUNNE

b. 1956

THE SMELL OF CAKE

I love the smell of cake in kitchens,
To stand in the heat of work and feel
The air warm as baked stones.
Dough clings to wooden spoons and bowls,
The worn edges of an old recipe book.
And your hair is powdered with flour,
Your palms smooth as a washed baking-board.
Above all, I love the finish when, together
Under the calendar that's months behind,
We swop spoons from a basin of cream and lick,
My beard flecked with it, your chin white,
And between us our son yelling for a lick,
And rising all around, the smell of rich, cooked cake.

AIDAN CARL MATHEWS

b. 1956

SPECTRUM

Everything we stand up in,
Worn long enough, makes one load:
Our warm, discoloured underwear,
The shirts off our backs,
Or the rose-bordered bedsheets
We have made and must lie upon.
On washdays, we entrust it all,
This fabric of our lives together,
To the darkened floodwaters
Of a cycle marked *delicates*.
I think often how you sat up
The first night that we got it,
New to the heavy, heart-like churning
Of its cold wash and its warm wash;
And I think of the silence after:
A turning, a total immersion.
In the reddish glow of the pilot,
Your white hands at the dials.
Tonight the clotheshorse fills
Like the makeshift sails on liferafts
In those B-movies that show
Two stowaways waking
Bone-dry and uninjured
Among cockatoos and banana-crops.
I am trying to say that our lives
Are running into each other
Like the dyes from separates.
You see it in the wash:
My vests the pink of nappy rash
From a royal blue blouse,
And your whitest pair of trousers

Ruined for good, with stains
The colour of flesh and blood
From something I slipped in
Among our sustaining garments,
Watermarks water won't budge.

ANDREW ELLIOTT

b. 1961

ANGEL

I think to make love to a nurse would be perfect,
Every germ and virus swimming in her mind
Like a kaleidoscope moving

Under a patient's skin,
Her breasts having nightmares of cancer,
Her hands like bowls weighing the ghosts of diseases.

Because she cannot control what she sees
Her body has turned inside out in the way she talks,
And left me, like a willing unfortunate,

To make my love nest
Among imaginary glands
And strange passageways,

The pink and white tissues of her genitals;
Unvaccinated and tempting fate
By bedding down with the untouchables,

Loving everything that happens under her skin.

ACKNOWLEDGEMENTS

Grateful acknowledgement is made to:

Anvil Press Poetry Ltd for permission to reprint poems from *The Non-Aligned Storyteller* (1984) by Thomas McCarthy;

Samuel Beckett, John Calder (Publishers) Ltd and The Grove Press for permission to reprint a poem from *Collected Poems in English and French* (1972);

Eavan Boland for permission to reprint poems from *The War Horse* (Victor Gollancz, 1975);

Sandra Buchanan for permission to reprint poems from *Inside Traffic* by George Buchanan (Carcanet, 1976);

Campbell Thomson & McLaughlin Ltd for permission to reprint poems from *Collected Poems* by W. R. Rodgers (Oxford University Press, 1971);

Carcanet Press Ltd for permission to reprint poems from *New & Selected Poems* by Anthony Cronin (Carcanet Press/Raven Arts Press, 1982);

Ceolfrith Press for permission to reprint a poem from *The Broken Circle* (1981) by Richard Kell;

The estate of the late Austin Clarke for permission to reprint poems from *Collected Poems* (Dolmen Press, 1974);

The estate of the late Padraic Colum for permission to reprint poems from *The Poet's Circuits* (Oxford Univesity Press, 1960);

Seamus Deane for permission to reprint poems from *Gradual Wars* (Irish University Press, 1972) and *Rumours* (Dolmen Press, 1977);

Dedalus Press for permission to reprint poems from *In Praise of Warmth* (1987) by Richard Kell and *I Bailed Out at Ardee* (1987) by Tom MacIntyre;

The estate of the late Denis Devlin for permission to reprint poems from *Collected Poems* (Dolmen Press, 1964);

Seán Dunne for permission to reprint a poem from *Against the Storm* (Dolmen Press, 1985);

Paul Durcan for permission to reprint poems from *The Selected Paul Durcan* and *The Berlin Wall Café* (Blackstaff Press, 1982 and 1985);

Andrew Elliott for permission to reprint a poem from *Trio 4* (Blackstaff Press, 1985);

Faber and Faber Ltd for permission to reprint poems and extracts from *The Hungry Grass* (1947) by Donagh MacDonagh; *Collected Poems* (1966) by Louis MacNeice; *High Island* (1974) and *The Price of Stone* (1985) by Richard Murphy; *Wintering Out* (1972), *Field Work* (1979) and *The Haw Lantern* (1987) by Seamus Heaney; *The Strange Museum* (1980) by Tom Paulin; *New Weather* (1973), *Why Brownlee Left* (1980) and *Quoof* (1983) by Paul Muldoon;

The estate of the late Padraic Fallon for permission to reprint a poem from *Poems* (Dolmen Press, 1974);

Peter Fallon on behalf of Katherine Kavanagh for permission to reprint poems from *Collected Poems* by Patrick Kavanagh (MacGibbon & Kee, 1964);

Peter Fallon for permission to reprint 'Carolina';

Farrar, Straus & Giroux, Inc., for permission to reprint poems from *Poems 1965–1975* © 1966, 1969, 1972, 1975, 1980, *Field Work* © 1976, 1979 and *The Haw Lantern* © 1987 by Seamus Heaney;

Padraic Fiacc for permission to reprint a poem from *The Selected Padraic Fiacc* (Blackstaff Press, 1979);

Michael Foley for permission to reprint an extract from *True Life Love Stories* and a poem from *The Go Situation* (Blackstaff Press, 1976 and 1982);

Gallery Press for permission to reprint poems and extracts from *In the Light on the Stones* (1978) by Francis Harvey; *Selected Poems* (1982) by Pearse Hutchinson; *Selected Poems 1956–1986* (1986) by James Simmons; *A Limerick Rake* (1978) by Desmond O'Grady; *Antarctica* (1985) by Derek Mahon and *Minding Ruth* (1983) by Aidan Carl Mathews;

Monk Gibbon for permission to reprint poems from *The Velvet Bow and Other Poems* (Martin Secker & Warburg Ltd, 1972);

The estate of the late John Hewitt for permission to reprint poems from *Out of My Time* and *Time Enough* (Blackstaff Press, 1974 and 1976);

Brendan Kennelly for permission to reprint poems from *New and Selected Poems* (Gallery Press, 1976);

Thomas Kinsella for permission to reprint poems from *Selected Poems 1956–1968* (Dolmen Press, 1973);

Michael Longley for permission to reprint poems from *Poems 1963–1983* (Salamander Press/Gallery Press, 1985);

The estate of the late Patrick MacDonagh for permission to reprint 'Be Still as You are Beautiful' and 'She Walked Unaware';

David Marcus for permission to reprint extracts from *The Midnight Court* by Brian Merriman, translated by David Marcus (Dolmen Press, 1966);
Martin Brian & O'Keeffe Ltd for permission to reprint poems from *Man on the Porch: Selected Poems* (1980) by Patrick Galvin;
Menard Press and Advent Books for permission to reprint an extract from *Dánta Grádha* (1975) by Augustus Young;
John Montague and Harold Matson Co., Inc., for permission to reprint poems from *Selected Poems* (Dolmen Press, 1982);
Eiléan Ní Chuilleanáin for permission to reprint 'Lay Your Arms Aside';
Julie O'Callaghan for permission to reprint a poem from *Edible Anecdotes* (Dolmen Press, 1983);
Seán Ó Tuama for permission to reprint a poem from *Poets of Munster: An Anthology* (Brandon Books/Anvil Press Poetry, 1985);
Oxford University Press for permission to reprint poems from *Poems 1962–1978* (1979) by Derek Mahon, and *The Flower Master* (1982) and *Venus and the Rain* (1984) by Medbh McGuckian;
William Peskett and Martin Secker & Warburg Ltd for permission to reprint poems from *The Night-owl's Dissection* (1975) and *Survivors* (1980);
A.D. Peters & Co. Ltd and Joan Daves for permission to reprint an extract and poems from *Kings, Lords and Commons: An Anthology from the Irish* (Macmillan, 1961) and *The Little Monasteries* (Dolmen Press, 1963), © 1959 by Frank O'Connor;
Raven Arts Press for permission to reprint poems from *Collected Poems, vol. 1* (1985) by Michael Hartnett, and *Selected Poems* (1986) by Nuala Ní Dhómhnaill, translated by Michael Hartnett;
Martin Secker & Warburg Ltd for permission to reprint poems from *Europa and the Bull* (1952) by W.R. Rodgers;
Joe Sheerin for permission to reprint poems from *A Crack in the Ice* (Dolmen Press, 1985);
Janet Shepperson for permission to reprint a poem from *Trio 5* (Blackstaff Press, 1987);
Wake Forest University Press for permission to reprint poems from *High Island* (1974) and *The Price of Stone* (1985) by Richard Murphy, and *New Weather* (1973), *Why Brownlee Left* (1980) and *Quoof* (1983) by Paul Muldoon;

A.P. Watt Ltd on behalf of Michael B. Yeats and Macmillan London Ltd, and Macmillan Publishing Co., for permission to reprint poems from *The Collected Poems of W. B. Yeats* (1937).

The publishers have made every effort to trace and acknowledge copyright holders. We apologise for any omissions in the above list and we will welcome additions or amendments to it for inclusion in any reprint edition.

INDEX OF FIRST LINES AND TITLES